The Business Valuation Bench Book

William J. Morrison
Jay E. Fishman

BVR
What It's Worth
1000 SW Broadway, Suite 1200, Portland, OR 97205
(503) 291-7963 • www.bvresources.com

The authors wish to acknowledge Jeremy C. Smith, ASA, and Lisa Cruikshank, ASA, both managing directors at Financial Research Associates, for their contributions to this publication.

BVR
What It's Worth

Publisher/Editor: Sarah Andersen

Executive Legal Editor: Sylvia Golden

Managing Editor: Monique Nijhout-Rowe

Senior Copy Editor: David Solomon

Chair and CEO: David Foster

President: Lucretia Lyons

Chief Revenue Officer: Lisa McInturff

Customer Service Manager: Retta Dodge

ISBN: 978-1-62150-110-7

EPUB ISBN: 978-1-62150-111-4

Library of Congress Control Number: 2017939756

To Shannon P. Pratt who led the way.

—Jay E. Fishman, 2017

I dedicate this book to my mother Maureen Morrison,
who at 96 continues to inspire and amaze.

—William J. Morrison, 2017

Table of Contents

Author Biographies

William J. Morrison, CPA/ABV, CFF, is a partner in the Paramus, N.J., office of WithumSmith+Brown. He is a certified public accountant in New Jersey and is accredited in business valuation and forensics by the American Institute of Certified Public Accountants (AICPA). He is a member of the firm's Litigation, Valuation and Insolvency Group.

Morrison founded and was president of the forensic accounting firm, Morrison & Co. (merged with WS+B in December 2010). He has over 35 years of experience as an investigator, forensic accountant, and business valuator. He has served as a special agent for the Federal Bureau of Investigation (FBI), an internal auditor, and a certified public accountant. Morrison has been qualified as an expert for the Supreme Court, Superior Court, and Federal Court of New Jersey and has been appointed as an expert for the federal and state courts in New Jersey in hundreds of matters as a forensic accountant, valuation expert, and mediator. He has provided expert witness services in complex civil and criminal matters involving stockholder oppression; high net worth divorces; economic damage claims; and federal, criminal, and tax matters, among others.

He has lectured to organizations such as The New Jersey Institute of Continuing Legal Education, American Society of Appraisers, National Association of Certified Valuation Analysts (NACVA), and the New Jersey Society of Certified Public Accountants (NJSCPA) on topics such as the maintenance of attorney trust accounts and forensic accounting. He has published numerous articles on business valuation and forensic accounting for *Fairshare, Valuing Professional Practices and Licenses,* and the *Encyclopedia of Matrimonial Practice.* He is the co-author with Jay Fishman and

Shannon Pratt of *Standards of Value, Theory and Application.*

A graduate of Boston College with a Bachelor of Arts degree in history, he also earned his master's degree in business administration from Fairleigh Dickinson University. He is a member of the AICPA, NJSCPA, and the Society of the Former Agents of the Federal Bureau of Investigation.

Jay E. Fishman, FASA, is a managing director of Financial Research Associates and has been actively engaged in the appraisal profession since 1974. He specializes in the valuations of business enterprises and their intangible assets. Fishman has co-written several books, including the highly acclaimed *Guide to Business Valuations* (with Shannon Pratt and James Hitchner) and *Standards of Value* (with Shannon Pratt and William Morrison). He has also written numerous articles on business valuations as well as qualifying as an expert witness and providing testimony in 12 states. He has taught courses on business valuation to the Internal Revenue Service, the National Judicial College, the Hong Kong Society of Accountants, and on behalf of the World Bank in St. Petersburg, Russia. He recently taught courses in Moscow, Russia, for Kwinto Management and for the Slovenian Institute of Auditors in Ljubljana, Slovenia.

He holds a bachelor's and master's degree from Temple University as well as an MBA from LaSalle University. Fishman is a Fellow of the American Society of Appraisers, a Fellow of the Royal Institution of Chartered Surveyors, a former chairman of the Business Valuation Committee of the American Society of Appraisers, editor of the *Business Valuation Review*, an editorial advisory board member of *Business Valuation Update*, chair of ASA's Government Relations Committee, a former trustee of The Appraisal Foundation, and is a member of the Appraisal Standards Board of The Appraisal Foundation. He finished his term as a member of the Appraisal Practice Board of The Appraisal Foundation in July 2016. He recently was awarded the Chairman's Public Service Award from The Appraisal Foundation. The award was established in 2005 to recognize individuals who have worked with the foundation for the benefit of the appraisal profession and who, in the process, have gone above and beyond the call of duty. Fishman was recently appointed as a member of the board of trustees of the International Valuation Standards Council (IVSC).

INTRODUCTION

In many judicial proceedings, especially those involving domestic and corporate disputes, the value of a closely held business or business interests is often the center of controversy. The process by which these businesses or business interests are valued can involve what appear to be arcane approaches, methods, and procedures. As such, these issues often result in the battle of the experts, all of whom seem to have, at least on paper, impressive résumés. The opposing experts may both seem credible yet reach wildly different conclusions. These issues are presented to judges who often have limited or no specialized training or experience dealing with these kinds of valuation issues but are asked to make findings on reports and testimony of these business valuation experts.

First, this book should serve as a reference guide of fundamental business valuation concepts. We present practical guidance on the concepts used in the business valuation process, including: standards of value, premises of value, adjustments to income, expenses, and approaches and methods of value. Within the valuation process, there are critical components including "normalized earnings," income to capitalize, the capitalization rate, and tax effects. Each expert makes judgments as to how he or she handles these critical components, which can lead to very different conclusions of value. *Second, we present a process whereby the trier of fact can separate a complex valuation into its component parts and analyze the expert's factual and theoretical support for his or her conclusions.*

For each section of this bench book, we present the main concepts in a bulleted format followed by a detailed explanation and charts, which the court can use to compare the critical components of each expert's report and the judgments he or she used to reach his or her conclusion of value. We also present case studies of a clothing store and a real estate holding company to further illustrate these concepts.

Additionally, we show, through examples, how even small changes in the critical components affect the conclusion of value. In each section, we present "Questions to Ask" to inquire as to the underlying facts and reasoning behind the expert's judgments and opinion.

We also include 12 appendices that can be photocopied and kept for easy reference. Appendix 1 is a reference chart on goodwill jurisprudence by state. Appendices 2 through 8 are blank charts that can be used to dissect and compare the experts' opinions on the critical components of their valuation. Appendix 9 explains discounts for lack of control and lack of marketability. Appendix 10 provides a glossary of valuation terms. Appendix 11 presents questions to ask experts, and Appendix 12 is a reference guide to important valuation concepts. Hopefully, this book will assist the court, as the trier of fact, make the findings necessary to reach a decision on the value of a business or business interest.

This book is written by two well-known valuation specialists from their perspective and should not be construed as providing legal advice. We wrote this book to provide a resource that can be used as a handy reference. It is by no means an exhaustive treatise on this subject, and there may be exceptions. Readers who are confronted with such exceptions should expect more thorough explanations of the reasons for the variances from their experts.

The authors would like to acknowledge the contributions of Christina Giorgio and Linda Cooke of WithumSmith+Brown for their valuable administrative assistance on this book.

LEARNING OBJECTIVES:

1. Be able to assess the facts, analysis, and judgments made by the business valuation experts and the conclusions they draw.

2. Understand:

   a. The terms "standard of value" and "premise of value" and how the standard of value affects the conclusion of value.

   b. Approaches to valuing a business:
      i. Market;
      ii. Income; and
      iii. Asset-based.

   c. Critical components of a business valuation, including:
      i. Normalized earnings adjustments:
         - Revenue;
         - Expense; and
         - Reasonable compensation.
      ii. Income to capitalize;
      iii. Tax effects;
      iv. Capitalization rate:
         - Discount rate; and
         - Growth rate.

3. Be able to compare and critique expert reports.
   i. Questions to ask
   ii. Degree of judgment in the experts' opinion
   iii. Effect these judgments have on the conclusion of value

Chapter 1. Business Valuation Concepts

POINTS COVERED IN THIS CHAPTER

Premises of Value:

- **Value in exchange:**
  Owner realizes the benefits of ownership by selling the business.

- **Value to the holder:**
  Owner realizes the benefits of ownership by the cash flow* received while owning the business.

Standards of Value:

- **Fair market value:**
  Value in exchange concept. The business is valued assuming a hypothetical sale between a willing buyer and a willing seller if appropriate minority and marketability discounts are allowed.

- **Fair value:**
  Can be similar to fair market value, but minority and marketability discounts are not typically applied. Can include the value to the holder premise because the business cannot be sold or there is no intention to sell.

* Cash flow is anything of monetary value that the owner benefits from in excess of reasonable compensation. This could include salary in excess of reasonable compensation, profits retained, distributions, perquisites, and other similar items.

When the value of a business or business interest is part of a dispute, the court will be asked to rule on the value of the business. In the matrimonial part, when one spouse has title to the business, the business is valued so that the nontitled spouse can receive his or her share in equitable distribution. In the general equity part, when there is a dispute among the owners of a business or the beneficiaries of an estate that own a business, the business is valued so that the owners can receive their fair share.

To most people, the question "what is my business worth?" is usually answered in terms of what it can be sold for on the market. However, when the court is asked to determine the value of a business, it is usually not afforded the luxury of exposing the business to the market for sale. A judge is being asked to figure out the worth of a business that is not actually being sold. This is a difficult task that requires the use of various assumptions. The valuation process involves questions such as: To whom would the business be sold? Would it be sold for cash or stock? How long will it take to sell? The answers to these questions are all wrapped up in the opinion of value.

The process begins with the consideration of the overarching premise of value, which represents the general concepts of property under which the standard of value falls. The two fundamental premises of value are value to the holder and value in exchange. Under value to the holder, the owner realizes the benefits of ownership by the cash flow received while owning the business. Under value in exchange, the owner realizes the benefits of ownership by selling the business.

In a judicial context, certain standards or definitions of value have been used to set the framework in attempts to answer these questions. The best known of these standards is *fair market value,* which comes from federal estate and gift tax matters. It is a *value in exchange* concept, wherein the business is valued assuming a hypothetical sale between a willing buyer and a willing seller. Under this standard, typically the entire business is valued, and, where applicable, lack of control and marketability discounts are applied to reduce the pro rata share of the business value.[1]

Another judicial standard of value is *fair value,* which is the standard used in cases involving dissenting or oppressed minority shareholders. This standard is state-specific and follows state statutes and case law. Since in many instances the majority owners

1 A discount for lack of control (or minority discount) is an amount or percentage deducted from the pro rata share of 100% of the value of an equity interest in a business to reflect the absence of some or all of the powers of control. A discount for lack of marketability (marketability discount) is an amount or percentage deducted from the value of an ownership interest to reflect the relative absence of marketability.

will likely purchase the interest of the dissenting or oppressed minority shareholders, courts have often determined that it would not be "fair" to allow the majority owners to purchase the minority shareholders' interest at a discount. "Fair" as used in this context is designed to give the dissenting or oppressed shareholders what has been taken from them: their pro rata share of the value of the business as a going concern.

Thus, in estate and gift matters, the courts apply fair market value with shareholder-level minority and marketability discounts if applicable. In dissent and oppression matters, fair value is generally applied without minority and marketability discounts. In divorce matters as in dissent and oppression cases, the individual state statutes and case law govern the standard of value. With a few exceptions, the statutes do not provide guidance as to the appropriate standard of value; one has to look to case law. However, the case law often does not provide clear guidance. For instance, more than 30 states reference fair market value in their case law but apply it differently. In this context, one of the biggest issues the states address is whether to include personal goodwill as a marital asset. See Appendix 1 for "Charting Goodwill Jurisprudence," which addresses how the courts have ruled on this issue in individual states. If the case law does not include personal goodwill as a marital asset because it is personal to an individual and cannot be sold, this implies a value in exchange premise of value and a fair market value standard of value.

Often choosing the appropriate standard of value is not a clear-cut issue. For instance, in dissent and oppression matters, most states do not allow for shareholder-level minority and marketability discounts, but several states, including New Jersey, Minnesota, and Connecticut, consider marketability discounts under extraordinary circumstances. We address these issues in great depth in *Standards of Value, Theory and Applications,* which we co-wrote with Shannon Pratt.

QUESTIONS TO ASK:

1. What is the expert's premise of value and what is his or her basis for following a value in exchange or value to the holder premise of value?
2. Was this the expert's choice or was the expert using a particular standard of value as directed by counsel?
3. Under the facts and circumstances of the case, has the expert chosen the correct premise of value and standard of value?

Chapter 2. Approaches to Value

POINTS COVERED IN THIS CHAPTER

Each of these approaches can be viewed in terms of the sale of your house:

- **Market approach**
  If you sell your house, you look at sales of houses similar to yours and make adjustments for amenities and other differences to arrive at an asking price. This is known in the valuation of real property as the sales comparison approach.

- **Income approach**
  If you rent your house, you can determine the value of your house by estimating the total rental income the house could generate over the years, assuming that a dollar today is worth more than a dollar in the future.

- **Asset-based approach**
  If you were to buy a new house, the builder would charge for the price of the land, the costs to construct the house, and a profit. This is referred to in the valuation of real property as the cost approach.

The valuation of a closely held or privately owned business or business interest is similar to the valuation of real property. If you were interested in selling your house, what would you do? You would look at recent sales of houses similar to yours and make adjustments for amenities and other differences in arriving at an asking price. In real property, that approach is called the sales comparison approach because you are using sales of similar properties to estimate the value of your house. In business valuation, the approach is similar and is called the *market approach*. However, because there is no apparent ready market for closely held businesses, one cannot look to the price at which his or her neighbor's business sold to make such a sales comparison.

Sometimes people rent houses. This produces rental income for the owner. If one estimated the total rental income a house would generate over the years and considered that a dollar today is worth more than a dollar in the future, the value of your house could be determined. This is termed the *income approach* in both the valuation of real property and businesses and business interests.

Lastly, if one were to buy a new house, the builder would charge for the price of the land and the costs to construct the house plus a profit. In real property, that way of determining value is known as the cost approach, and, in business valuation, it is known as the *asset-based approach*.

QUESTIONS TO ASK:

1. Has the expert considered the market, income, and asset approaches?
2. What is his or her support for using one approach over the other?
3. Why were certain approaches excluded?

Factors to Consider

The Eight Factors of Revenue Ruling 59-60:

1. Nature and history of the business;
2. Economic and industry conditions;
3. Book value and financial condition;
4. Earning capacity;
5. Dividend-paying capacity;
6. Goodwill or other intangible value;
7. Prior sales of the stock and percentage of the business being valued; and
8. Market price for corporations in the same, or similar, line of business.

To make the judgments necessary to value a business, the expert needs to be well-informed about the business, the economy, and the industry in which the business operates. He or she also needs to consider all relevant factors and apply the methods appropriate to the particular company at that particular time and circumstance. In 1959, the Internal Revenue Service produced Revenue Ruling 59-60 (RR 59-60). This document provides basic guidelines that the financial expert should consider when valuing a closely held business or business interest. A revenue ruling is not the law but is the IRS's position relative to certain matters. In the case of Revenue Ruling 59-60, it is the IRS's position with regard to the valuation of business and business interests in connection with estate and gift tax matters. However, given its practical advice, Revenue Ruling 59-60 is a universally used benchmark by business appraisers. The Revenue Ruling states that:

> In valuing the stock of closely held corporations or the stock of corporations where market quotations are not available, all other available financial data, as well as all relevant factors affecting the fair market value must be considered for estate tax and gift tax purposes. *No general formula may be given that is applicable to the many different valuation situations arising in the valuation of such stock.* However, the general approach, methods, and factors which must be considered in valuing such securities are outlined (IRS Revenue Ruling 59-60).

The RR 59-60 directs the financial expert to consider the following eight factors:

> Has the expert considered the eight factors of RR 59-60?

1. The nature of the business and the history of the enterprise from its inception;
2. The economic outlook in general and the condition and outlook of the specific industry in particular;
3. The book value of the stock and the financial condition of the business;
4. The earning capacity of the company;
5. The dividend-paying capacity;
6. Whether or not the enterprise has goodwill or other intangible value;
7. Sales of the stock and the size of the block of stock to be valued; and
8. The market price of stocks of corporations engaged in the same or a similar line of business having their stocks actively traded in a free and open market, either on an exchange or over the counter.

Moreover, section 7 of RR 59-60 states:

> Because valuations cannot be made on the basis of a prescribed formula, there is no means whereby the various applicable factors in a particular case can be assigned mathematical weights in deriving the fair market value. For this reason, no useful purpose is served by taking an average of several factors (for example, book value, capitalized earnings and capitalized dividends) and basing the valuation on the result. Such a process excludes active consideration of other pertinent factors, and the end result cannot be supported by a realistic application of the significant facts in the case except by mere chance.

> Usually, the expert who understands the business best is the one who is most able to make sound valuation judgments.

While not all inclusive, the basic guidelines, including the eight factors of RR 59-60, are universally recognized as an apt starting point in valuing a closely held business or business interest. In the following chapters, we explain the income approach, the asset-based approach, the market approach, and the hybrid excess-earnings method.

This method is termed a hybrid method because it uses aspects of both the income and asset approaches. The methodologies you will see most often under these three approaches will be either a version of the income approach and/or the excess-earnings method. For this reason, we begin with the income approach followed by the asset approach, the excess-earnings method, and lastly, the market approach. Each of these approaches involves judgment by the expert.

When the expert makes seemingly small changes in critical components, these changes can have a large effect on the conclusion of value.

QUESTIONS TO ASK:

1. Does the expert have a thorough understanding of the business?
2. Has the expert considered the eight factors of Revenue Ruling 59-60?

Chapter 3. Income Approach

POINTS COVERED IN THIS CHAPTER

- Value is the present worth of future benefits of ownership.
- The present value of a dollar ($1) today is worth more than $1 in the future.

Although we have indicated that three valuation approaches are acceptable, in theory, all valuation approaches and methods are based on the concept that value is the present worth of future benefits. Under the income approach, there are two valuation methods: the income capitalization method and the discounted cash flow method. They are essentially the same but present the information differently and are used under different circumstances.

At a 5% interest factor, $1 today will be worth $1.05 in one year. Consequently, $1.05 payable in one year is worth $1 today and $0.95 paid in one year is worth $0.90 today.

Income Capitalization Method

POINTS COVERED IN THIS SECTION

- Used when the expected future income or cash flow can be determined as one normalized amount, which will grow at an average annual rate, for instance, 3%.
- Value is calculated as:

Value = income/cap rate

Let us begin with the income capitalization method. This method is used when the expected future income, or cash flow, can be determined as one normalized amount, which will grow at a constant average annual rate, for example, 3%. This usually occurs when the business and/or the economic conditions that affect the business have stabilized. If the expected future income will grow erratically or at varying amounts, or grow rapidly and then level off, or if the income will decrease, the discounted cash flow, or DCF, method would be more appropriate. The DCF method is more complex and will be discussed later.

In the income capitalization method, the expert calculates value by dividing income by a capitalization rate (cap rate). Cap rates are more fully described starting on page 38. Theoretically, the cap rate converts the future economic benefits of a business to their present value through the use of a divisor (%) or a multiplier. The application of this method requires a certain degree of judgment about *critical components,* including normalized earnings, income to capitalize, tax effects, and the capitalization rate. In this methodology, value can be calculated with a divisor where:

Value = income/cap rate

Where the financial expert determines that the income to capitalize equals $180,000 and the cap rate is 20%, the value equals $900,000:

$900,000 = $180,000/20%

The cap rate, which is a divisor, can also be expressed as a multiplier. The P/E[1] ratio is a multiplier that is used in the valuation of publicly traded stocks. In this case, the P/E ratio would be 5, which is calculated by dividing the cap rate into 100 (100/20 = 5):

$900,000 = $180,000 × 5

The following are examples of P/E ratios for publicly traded stocks as of June 30, 2016, and the implied cap rates:

	P/E ratios	Implied cap rates
International Business Machines (IBM)	11.52	8.68%
Coca-Cola Co.	27.28	3.67%
Apple Inc.	10.62	9.42%

1 Price to earnings.

The court will hear some experts use multipliers instead of cap rates. For illustration purposes, multiples of 1 to 5, and their corresponding cap rates, are shown in the chart below.

Cap Rate		Multiple
100%	=	1
50%	=	2
33.33%	=	3
25%	=	4
20%	=	5

It is very important for the expert to match the income and the cap rate. Different levels of income, i.e. pretax income, EBITDA,[2] or net income logically require different cap rates. Books have been written on how to calculate the income to capitalize and how to calculate the cap rate. We will now discuss how experts estimate "normalized income"[3] and "cap rates."

Has the appraiser matched the income to the cap rate?

In the income capitalization method, the expert will:

1. Make normalized earnings adjustments:
   a. Revenue;
   b. Expense; and
   c. Reasonable compensation.

2. Determine income to capitalize;

3. Determine the tax effect;

4. Determine an appropriate capitalization rate:
   a. Discount rate; and
   b. Growth rate.

QUESTIONS TO ASK

1. Has the expert matched the income to the cap rate?

2. Do they make common sense?

2 Earnings before interest, tax, depreciation, and amortization.

3 Income is used generically here. It is, essentially, economic benefits and may be income before or after taxes or cash flow. Free cash flow is defined as after-tax income plus depreciation and amortization less capital expenditures and working capital. The appraiser will need to explain the measure of economic benefits he or she has chosen and match it to the cap rate. For simplicity purposes, we are using income and cash flow interchangeably. The preferred benefit is free cash flow.

NORMALIZED EARNINGS

POINTS COVERED IN THIS SECTION

- Most closely held business owners attempt to minimize taxes;
- They typically pay themselves what the business can afford to pay and typically report little, if any, earnings;
- Closely held businesses normally distribute profits as salary and other benefits;
- Public companies maximize profits and distribute them to shareholders as dividends; and
- Therefore, the expert adjusts the financial statements to show earnings as if the business were run by a third party whose goal was to maximize profit, not to minimize taxes. In other words, the expert adjusts the income as if the owner is preparing to sell the company.

The first step in determining the income to capitalize is to normalize earnings. Closely held businesses do not typically have the same number of shareholders as publicly traded companies, nor are they scrutinized by the Securities and Exchange Commission like publicly traded companies. Accordingly, most closely held business owners attempt to minimize taxes. Closely held businesses pay the owner what the business can afford to pay and typically report little, if any, earnings. Public companies distribute profits as dividends. Closely held businesses often distribute profits as excess salary and other benefits to the owner.

During the valuation process, the expert analyzes the books and records of the subject company and makes adjustments to the earnings as if the business were run by third-party (nonowner) management. Adjustments are made for items including discretionary personal expenses, nonrecurring expenses, extraordinary expenses, as well as extraordinary income and nonrecurring income items—and, of course, unreported income. The expert should be able to explain each adjustment to you and perform the analysis the same way whether the husband or the wife is his or her client.

Simply put, the reported historical performance of the business may look different if it were run by third-party management or being prepared for sale. It is the expert's role to adjust this information as if the business were run by a third party whose goal was to maximize profit, not to minimize taxes. The normalization process is also performed in the discounted cash flow method, the excess earnings method, and the methods used in the market approach.

The expert should be able to explain the reasons for his or her adjustments in an understandable manner.

The expert begins his or her financial analysis by obtaining tax returns and/or financial statements for a period of years, usually five, prior to the valuation date. The expert analyzes these documents and conducts a review of the financial statements and the underlying books and records of the company, the overall economy, and the condition and outlook for the specific industry in which the business operates. The experts should attempt to gain insight also from the owner, the nonowner spouse, and other knowledgeable individuals, either by voluntary interview or, if necessary, deposition. Based on this review, the expert makes adjustments to the information reported on the tax returns or financial statements so that expenses that are not necessary to operate the business are removed. The expert's goal in making these adjustments is to calculate the normalized earnings, or free cash flow, of the company. *When the court reviews an appraisal report or listens to testimony, the court should note the adjustments made by each expert and see where and why they differ in their adjustments.*

The following are examples of typical adjustments the expert makes to the revenues and expenses of the business.

Adjustments to Revenue

POINTS COVERED IN THIS SECTION

- Most adjustments will increase income;
- Examples of adjustments to revenue include:
  - Unreported cash or other proceeds;
  - Deferred revenue—the net change for each year is what is important; and
  - Nonrecurring revenue.

Typically, most adjustments will increase income. One of the most provocative adjustments the expert makes is to add cash or other funds to the company's revenues when he or she believes the company has not reported these funds. However, finding unreported revenue can be difficult and time-consuming. Experts are rarely able to prove the amounts definitively, and their adjustments should be carefully reviewed because an expert should not make these adjustments without evidence. Owners can also defer revenue by including December revenue in the following January. Here, the expert may need to allocate between years, i.e., remove the December 2011 revenue reported in January 2012 and include the December 2012 revenue reported in January 2013. The expert should carefully consider income deferrals because it is the net change that is important. In other words, if the company held back revenue in 2011, it may have held back revenue in 2010; therefore, it is the difference that gets added to the 2011 income.

On the other hand, the expert could lower revenue for nonrecurring revenue items. For example, if a company made a one-time (i.e. nonrecurring) sale of $50,000, the expert could reduce revenue by this amount.

Adjustments to Expenses

POINTS COVERED IN THIS SECTION

- Most often, but not always, these adjustments increase income:
  - Personal expenses;
  - Nonrecurring expenses;
  - Extraordinary expenses; and
  - Normalization adjustments.

The expert will also make adjustments to expenses. Most often, but not always, these adjustments will increase income:

1. *Personal expenses*

   The owner may pay personal or other types of discretionary expenses through the business and deduct them from income. These expenses are removed and increase the entity's income.

2. *Nonrecurring expenses*
   If an expense is not expected to repeat, the expert could remove it. This would include a natural disaster or the loss of a product line. Typically, these adjustments increase earnings.

3. *Extraordinary expenses*
   The expert removes expenses for extraordinary events. For example, the costs of a hurricane or fire would be removed as extraordinary expenses.

4. *Normalization adjustments*
   The expert can make adjustments to normalize earnings. These adjustments can increase or decrease income. Assume the company had prepaid some accounting expenses in one year. That expense should be spread over two years to reflect the normal cost for each year.

QUESTIONS TO ASK

Revenues

1. Has unreported revenue been proven and included?
2. Have nonrecurring and one-time revenues been removed?
3. Is revenue included in proper time period?

Expenses

1. Have personal expenses been removed?
2. Have nonrecurring and extraordinary expenses been removed?
3. Are expenses allocated to the proper periods?

General

1. Can the expert explain the reasons for his or her adjustments?
2. Which expert has the more reasonable, understandable, and supportable adjustments?
3. Can each expert explain why his or her income statements after adjustments are more reasonable?

Reasonable Compensation

POINTS COVERED IN THIS SECTION

- Adjusts the amount paid to the owner to an amount that a nonowner employee would receive to perform the same services;
- Considers the age, experience, productivity, locale, education and expertise of the owner/employee, and the location of the business; and
- Often one of the biggest differences between two experts.

One of the principle characteristics of a closely held business is that its owners are often employed by the business. The expert should always consider an adjustment for reasonable compensation to adjust the amount paid to the owner to an amount that a nonowner employee would receive for performing the same services. The New Jersey Supreme Court has provided guidance for the factors to be considered to determine reasonable compensation. In determining the value of a law practice, the court outlined the task in assessing reasonable compensation as follows:

> *The court should first ascertain what an attorney of comparable experience, expertise, education and age would be earning as an employee in the same general locale.* The effort that the practitioner expends on his law practice should not be overlooked when comparing his income to that of the hypothetical employee. A sole practitioner, who, for example, works a regular 60-hour week, may have a significantly greater income than an employee who regularly works a 40-hour week, and the income may be due to greater productivity than the realization of income on the sole practitioner's goodwill. *Dugan v. Dugan,* 92 N.J. 423, 439 (1983) (emphasis added)

Although the aforementioned applies to a law practice, the general guidelines are applicable in determining replacement compensation for most closely held businesses. In determining reasonable compensation, the expert should consider the age, experience, productivity, education and expertise of the owner/employee, and the location of the business—in other words, what would be paid to a nonowner/employee performing the same services. This is an area where you may find one of the biggest differences between the two experts.

The adjustment for reasonable compensation is one of the most difficult judgments made in the valuation process. The court should expect the expert to be able to carefully explain the basis for this adjustment. Most experts consider a combination of factors, including compensation studies, salary structure of the target companies, and highest paid nonowner employees of the subject business.

QUESTIONS TO ASK

1. Does the compensation make sense?
2. Would a nonowner employee perform this work for this amount of money?
3. Can you hire a lawyer to work 60 hours a week, bill $500,000 a year, and manage the firm for a mere $80,000?
4. Has the expert considered the age, experience, productivity and expertise of the owner, and the location of the business to determine what the compensation would be to replicate the owner's services?

In our case study, we use a clothing store to apply the three valuation approaches including the excess earnings method. We will follow two experts (Expert No. 1 and Expert No. 2) in order to show the effect of the expert's individual judgments on his or her determination of value. These two experts present typical adjustments made when preparing business valuations. Expert No. 1 makes judgments that lower his or her value, while Expert No. 2's judgments increase his or her value. We begin with the normalized earnings adjustments and follow the two experts' judgments through the value calculations, including income to capitalize, tax effects, capitalization rate, discounted cash flow, net asset value method, excess earnings method, and the market approach.

CASE STUDY: NORMALIZED EARNINGS

The expert usually starts with either the tax returns or the financial statements of the company. In the first example, labeled Expert 1, reported sales are $1,750,000; the cost of goods sold equal $875,000. Cost of goods sold is the cost of the product the company is selling. These costs are subtracted from the sales to arrive at the gross profit. In a clothing store, the cost of goods sold would be the cost of the clothing being sold in the store. The operating expenses are all of other costs of running the business. In this example, the reported operating expenses equal $775,000. These are also subtracted from the sales to arrive at the income before taxes, which equals $100,000 ($1,750,000 - $875,000

- $775,000). Typically, reported income taxes are removed and the expert recalculates income taxes based on normalized earnings. The first expert makes seven adjustments to the expenses. These adjustments total $100,000, after which the income before taxes is increased to $200,000. Most experts use a format similar to the following to show the effect of their adjustments. *This is an area where many differences can be identified.*

EXPERT NO. 1

Expert No. 1 makes seven adjustments to increase income from $100,000 to $200,000.

	Income As Reported	Adjustments		Adjusted Income
Sales	$1,750,000	—	(a)	$1,750,000
Cost of Goods Sold				
Beginning Inventory	250,000			250,000
Purchases	695,000	($20,000)	(b)	675,000
Shipping & Freight	205,000			205,000
Ending Inventory	(275,000)			(275,000)
Total COGS	875,000			855,000
Gross Profit	875,000			895,000
Operating Expenses				
Advertising	3,500			3,500
Auto & Truck	20,000	(4,500)	(c)	15,500
Contributions	2,000	(2,000)	(d)	—
Employee Benefits	37,500	—	(e)	37,500
Insurance	42,500	(15,000)	(f)	27,500
Legal & Professional	25,000	—	(g)	25,000
Miscellaneous	4,500	(1,500)	(h)	3,000
Office	7,500			7,500
Rent	40,000			40,000
Repairs & Maintenance	25,000			25,000
Salaries	285,000			285,000
Utilities	17,500	(7,000)	(i)	10,500
Officer's Compensation	250,000	(50,000)	(j)	200,000
Depreciation	15,000			15,000
Amortization	—			—
Total Expenses	775,000			695,000
Income Before Taxes	**$100,000**	**($100,000)**		**$200,000**

The reasons[4] for these adjustments are as follows:

(a) *Unreported Income*—no adjustment.

(b) *Purchases*—after a review of the books and records of the company, we have deemed $20,000 of the purchases to be personal in nature.

(c) *Auto and truck*—after a review of the books and records and the interviews with the parties, we have added back $4,500 of the auto expense as personal in nature.

(d) *Contributions*—the contributions of $2,000 made were deemed to be discretionary in nature and, as a result, were added back.

(e) *Employee benefits*—no adjustment.

(f) *Insurance*—after a review of the books and records and the interviews with the parties, it was determined that the parties' personal homeowners insurance and car insurance were paid through the business. Therefore, $15,000 was deemed personal in nature and added back.

(g) *Legal and professional*—no adjustment.

(h) *Miscellaneous*—after a review of the miscellaneous transactions in the books and records, we have deemed $1,500 as personal in nature. These expenses have been added back.

(i) *Utilities*—after a review of the books and records and the interviews with the parties, we have deemed $7,000 of the utilities expense as personal in nature.

(j) *Reasonable compensation*—as a result of our review of the compensation studies and company records, we have added back $50,000 in officer's compensation and deemed $200,000 to be reasonable compensation.[5]

Typically, if there is more than one expert in the case, they will not agree on the amount or even the areas that require adjustments to normalize the earnings. Some of the adjustments are easy to analyze. Where personal expenses are alleged to have been paid through the business, what do the documents show? Was the insurance business or personal? In other instances, the issues are more subtle. Was the dinner business or personal? The expert needs to explain the reasoning for his or her adjustments. Often, the experts will differ on what the reasonable compensation of the owner should be. Each will cite studies and other types of information to support his or her opinion.

4 Although no adjustments were made for unreported income, employee benefits, and legal and professional fees, they were included for comparison to Expert No. 2, where adjustments are made for these categories.

5 An adjustment that must be considered in determining the earnings capacity of the company is that of reasonable compensation for the owner or owners. As mentioned previously, the compensation paid to the owner of a closely held company tends to be based on what the company can afford and may bear little relationship to the market value of the services actually performed. The reasonable compensation adjustment substitutes the cost of hiring and paying a nonowner employee to perform the same services performed by the owner.

EXPERT NO. 2

Expert No. 2 makes 10 adjustments to increase income from $100,000 to $300,000.

	Income As Reported	Adjustments		Adjusted Income
Sales	$1,750,000	$20,000	(a)	$1,770,000
Cost of Goods Sold				
Beginning Inventory	250,000			250,000
Purchases	695,000	(40,000)	(b)	655,000
Shipping & Freight	205,000			205,000
Ending Inventory	(275,000)			(275,000)
Total COGS	875,000			835,000
Gross Profit	875,000			935,000
Operating Expenses				
Advertising	3,500			3,500
Auto & Truck	20,000	(9,000)	(c)	11,000
Contributions	2,000	(2,000)	(d)	-
Employee Benefits	37,500	(13,000)	(e)	24,500
Insurance	42,500	(15,000)	(f)	27,500
Legal & Professional	25,000	(13,000)	(g)	12,000
Miscellaneous	4,500	(4,500)	(h)	-
Office	7,500			7,500
Rent	40,000			40,000
Repairs & Maintenance	25,000			25,000
Salaries	285,000			285,000
Utilities	17,500	(8,500)	(i)	9,000
Officer's Compensation	250,000	(75,000)	(j)	175,000
Depreciation	15,000			15,000
Amortization	-			-
Total Expenses	775,000			635,000
Income Before Taxes	**$100,000**	**($200,000)**		**$300,000**

The reasoning for these adjustments is as follows:

(a) *Unreported income*—after a review of the books and records and bank accounts, we have added an additional $20,000 in deposits as income.

(b) *Purchases*—after a review of the books and records, we have deemed $40,000 of the purchases reported as personal in nature.

(c) *Auto and truck*—after a review of the books and records and interviews with the parties, we have added back $9,000 of the auto expense as personal in nature.

(d) *Contributions*—the contributions of $2,000 made were deemed to be discretionary in nature and, as a result, were added back.

(e) *Employee benefits*—we have determined that the owner is the sole beneficiary of the pension and profit sharing expense. As a result, we added back the entire $13,000 in contributions.

(f) *Insurance*—after a review of the books and records and interviews with the parties, it was determined that the parties' homeowners and car insurance was paid through the business. Therefore, $15,000 was deemed personal in nature and added back.

(g) *Legal and professional*—we have deemed that $13,000 of the legal expenses is nonrecurring. As a result, we have added back $13,000.

(h) *Miscellaneous*—after a review of the miscellaneous transactions in the books and records, we have deemed the entire $4,500 as personal in nature. These expenses have been added back.

(i) *Utilities*—after a review of the books and records and the interviews with the parties, we have deemed $8,500 of the utilities expense as personal in nature.

(j) *Reasonable compensation*—as a result of our review of the resources available, we have added back $75,000 in officer's compensation and deemed $175,000 to be reasonable compensation.

At this point, the experts will have adjusted the financial statements of the company to present them as if an independent third party ran the business by normalizing earning through adjustments that:

1. Include unreported income;
2. Normalize deferred income;
3. Remove personal expenses;
4. Remove extraordinary income and expenses;
5. Remove nonrecurring income and expenses;
6. Present income and expenses in the proper time period; and
7. Adjust actual owner's compensation to reasonable compensation for the services performed.

Consider having the experts prepare a joint chart that compares their adjustments and highlights the differences. An example is presented below.

It is helpful to look at the revenues and expenses after adjustments to see whether they look reasonable. The expert should be able to explain whether the expenses he or she presents properly match the revenues. For instance, if the cost of goods sold are 50% for other companies in the industry, how does this company operate with a 30% cost of goods sold?

Which appraiser's adjustments position makes more sense?

In our case study, the experts normalized the income for one year. Typically, the expert will adjust the income for more than one year, often for five years. The purpose of looking at the company over time is to identify trends that will help indicate how the business will perform in the future.

The following chart presents the adjustments of Expert No. 1 and Expert No. 2 and includes a column for the judge to make his or her adjustments.

NORMALIZATION ADJUSTMENTS COMPARISON

	Expert No. 1	Expert No. 2	Judge
Income	$100,000	$100,000	$100,000
Add:			
Unreported income	-	20,000	
Personal purchases	20,000	40,000	
Auto & truck	4,500	9,000	
Contributions	2,000	2,000	
Employee benefits	-	13,000	
Insurance	15,000	15,000	
Legal & professional	-	13,000	
Miscellaneous	1,500	4,500	
Utilities	7,000	8,500	
Reasonable compensation	50,000	75,000	
Income before tax	$200,000	$300,000	

Attached as Appendix 2 is a blank normalization adjustment comparison chart. This allows for the comparison of experts' additions and subtractions to reported net income in an actual case. Additionally, the reasonable compensation adjustment is set forth in the traditional fashion in which the reported owner's compensation is added back to net income and the "reasonable compensation" is subtracted. In the above example, the reported owner's compensation was $250,000 and the reasonable compensation was $200,000 for Expert No. 1 and $175,000 for Expert No. 2. The adjustments were presented net at $50,000 for Expert No. 1 and $75,000 for Expert No. 2. Using the format in Appendix 2, the reasonable compensation adjustment would be set forth as follows:

	Expert No. 1	Expert No. 2	Judge
Reported owners compensation	$250,000	$250,000	$250,000
Less: reasonable compensation	($200,000)	($175,000)	

The net adjustment results from the computation but is not shown in the chart above.

INCOME TO CAPITALIZE

POINTS COVERED IN THIS SECTION

- Choose a period to capitalize. Some typical periods used are:
  - The most recent operations of the past 12 months or fiscal year;
  - A forecast (projection) of the next year;
  - An average of the operations for several past years; and
  - Median or average profit margins for the past several years.

The expert must now determine a normalized income level to capitalize. In this process, the expert attempts to determine the expected future earnings or cash flow of the business. The business's historical performance is used as a guide for the future. This can be done by looking at averages, weighted averages (where more weight is afforded certain years), net profit margins, or, in some instances, the most recent year's income. Some typical periods used are:

- The most recent operations of the past 12 months or fiscal year;
- A forecast (projection) of the next year;
- An average of the operations for several past years; and
- Median or average profit margins.

CASE STUDY: INCOME TO CAPITALIZE

To this point, we analyzed only the most recent year's income before tax. Expert No. 1 calculated income before tax of $200,000 and Expert No. 2, $300,000, for a difference of $100,000 in the income before tax to capitalize. The experts are attempting to estimate the expected future income, which can be done in any one of a number of different ways, including those explained above. Expert No. 1 believes a weighted five-year average in which the most recent year is given a weight of five (5) and the oldest year a weight of one (1) best estimates the expected future earnings. (For purposes of this analysis, we estimated the income for the four earlier years as set forth below.) Expert No. 2 believes the most recent year best estimates future earnings. Based on the choice of the income to capitalize the two experts made, the difference between the two experts increases. The $200,000 income Expert No. 1 used becomes $180,000 as compared to the $300,000 of Expert No. 2 as set forth below:

Year	Income	Weight	Weighted
2013	$200,000	5	$1,000,000
2012	180,000	4	720,000
2011	160,000	3	480,000
2010	175,000	2	350,000
2009	150,000	1	150,000
Total		15	2,700,000
Divided by			15
Income to Capitalize			$180,000

Therefore, income to capitalize for Expert No. 1 is a weighted average of $180,000 for the past five years, while, for Expert No. 2, it is the latest year's adjusted income before taxes of $300,000.

Why does the expert think these periods and weighting of historical results best represent the future?

What is the correct period to use? There is no right or wrong answer to this question, but the expert should try to predict whether the past is an accurate predictor of the future. For example, did the business lose a major customer or gain one? If the future is more like the past, a simple or weighted average, such as Expert No. 1 uses, may make sense. If the company has grown significantly and the future is more like the most recent past, the most recent year Expert No. 2 used may be more appropriate. The expert may even develop an expected profit percentage and use that percentage with his or her estimate of the expected future revenue.

Have the expert explain why he or she believes his or her determination of the income to capitalize best represents the future. He or she should be consistent with the facts. Why would a business that has been shrinking suddenly grow? Why would the income from four or five years ago be weighted or included in any fashion in a growing business? These questions require detailed explanations from the experts.

The critical components addressed so far are the normalized earnings adjustments[6] and the income to capitalize. The following is a sensitivity analysis, which demonstrates how changing two critical components changes the value of the company significantly. Using the 20% (0.20) cap rate with income of $180,000 from Expert No. 1 and $300,000 from Expert No. 2 produces the following values:

Income/Cap rate = Value

$$\frac{\$180{,}000}{0.2} \qquad \frac{\$300{,}000}{0.2}$$

$$\underline{\underline{\$900{,}000}} \qquad \underline{\underline{\$1{,}500{,}000}}$$

As demonstrated above, the value of $900,000 increases to $1,500,000 by increasing income from $180,000 to $300,000. Remember, value is calculated by "capitalizing" income (dividing income by a percentage). While this is not a small difference, even changing the income by a small amount can have a significant impact on value. In the above example, every $10,000 in additional income adds *$50,000* in value!

So far, we have examined the income in the formula:

Income/Cap rate = Value

6 These include adjustments to revenues, expenses, and reasonable compensation.

Tax Affecting the Income to Capitalize

POINTS COVERED IN THIS SECTION

- The buildup method used to calculate the cap rate is used with after-tax income; and
- Whether to tax affect the income of pass-through entities is a controversial issue in the valuation community.

Choosing whether to reduce the income to capitalize by federal and state taxes is the next critical component the expert needs to address. The expert "tax affects" the income to capitalize by deducting federal and state income taxes from the normalized income to capitalize. The buildup method used to calculate the cap rate described in the next section is used with after-tax income. Therefore, when using the buildup method, experts should tax affect income. As previously stated, the income to capitalize must be matched to the appropriate cap rate. Whether to tax affect the income of pass-through entities such as subchapter S corporations (S corp), partnerships, limited liability corporations (LLCs), and limited liability partnerships (LLPs) is a controversial issue in the valuation community. This section will address tax affecting in general and tax affecting of pass-through entities in particular.

Matching the Income to Capitalize and the Cap Rate

Assume that a business has the following income statement:

Revenues	$1,000,000
Cost of sales	(500,000)
Gross profit	500,000
Operating expenses	(166,667)
Pretax income	333,333
Taxes at 40%	(133,333)
After-tax income	$200,000

There is no rule that the income an expert capitalizes is pretax or after tax, but the income must be matched to the cap rate. When the cap rate is calculated using the buildup method (see the following section), the level of income to capitalize is after-tax income because this discount rate component of the cap rate is derived from the public markets and the public companies report their income after taxes. Therefore, if the after-tax income of a business is $200,000 and the expert determines that the cap rate is 20%, the value of the business would be $1,000,000—$200,000/20% = $1,000,000. Using pretax income, the cap rate would be 33.3% to arrive at the same value of $1,000,000. If revenues were being capitalized, the cap rate would be 100% to arrive at the same value ($1,000,000/100%). The value of a business should not change if the expert capitalizes pretax or after-tax income:[7]

After-tax income	$200,000/20% = $1,000,000
Pretax income	$333,333/33.3% = $1,000,000
Revenues	$1,000,000/100% = $1,000,000

Going From an After-Tax to Pretax Cap Rate

The mathematical relationship between a pretax and an after-tax cap rate is the same as the relationship between these two levels of income. In this case, the after-tax income is 60% of the pretax income ($200,000/$333,333 = 60%). To adjust the after-tax cap rate of 20% to a pretax cap rate, divide the after-tax cap rate by 60%, or 0.6 (20%/0.6 = 33.3%), or, if the tax rate is 33.3%, the pretax cap rate is calculated by dividing the after-tax cap rate by 0.67 (20%/0.67 = 30%).

The following is a conversion chart to adjust the after-tax cap rate to a pretax cap rate.

Tax Rate	After-tax Cap Rate	Pre-tax Cap Rate
25.0%	20.0%	26.7%
30.0%	20.0%	28.6%
33.3%	20.0%	30.0%
40.0%	20.0%	33.3%

While it is not improper to capitalize pretax income, the expert should choose a cap rate that reflects the risk associated with the pretax income and the relationship to an after-tax cap rate.

7 Although beyond the scope of this book, converting an after-tax capitalization rate to a pretax discount rate can be a complicated process. One must first convert the after-tax capitalization rate to a pretax rate and then add in the growth rate. This will provide a discount rate applicable to pretax cash flows.

PASS-THROUGH ENTITIES (PTE)

In accordance with Subchapter C of the Internal Revenue Code, corporations pay taxes on the income they report. Hence, they are referred to as C corporations. Then, when the C corporation pays a dividend to the stockholder, he or she pays income tax on the dividend income. Thus, the income is taxed twice: first, by the corporation, when it reports the income, and then by the shareholder, when he or she receives a dividend. This amounts to double taxation of the dividends. To avoid the double taxation of dividends[8] and other tax restrictions of the C corporation, certain corporations (typically smaller corporations with simple capital structures) can elect to have the shareholders report their income and losses in accordance with Subchapter S of the Internal Revenue Code. Corporations that elect to have their shareholders report and pay taxes on the corporate income are known as S corporations. This enables the S corp to act as a flow-through entity in that the owners report the business's income and losses on their personal tax returns, similar to partnerships, LLCs, or LLPs. The issue is whether the income of a flow-through entity should be tax affected in the capitalization of earnings, discounted cash flow, or excess earnings methods.

Two series of cases address this issue. The first is a tax court case, *Gross v. Commissioner,*[9] in which the Tax Court held that S corp income was not to be tax affected because the S corp did not pay income taxes. The individual shareholders pay taxes on the corporate income. The court did not want to compromise the tax rate and found the 0% tax rate of the IRS expert to be more credible than the 40% tax rate the taxpayer's expert chose. Since the actual tax rate in this case was 40%, this had the effect of increasing the value of the business by 67%.

	0% Tax Rate		**40% Tax Rate**
Pretax income	$333,333		$333,333
Less: taxes	-		(133,333)
After-tax income	333,333		200,000
Divided by: cap rate	20%		20%
Calculated value (rounded)	$1,667,000		$1,000,000
Difference	$667,000 / $1,000,000	=	67%

8 There are other benefits such as the ability of the stockholder to deduct corporate losses.
9 *Gross v. Commissioner*, T.C. Memo 1999-254, aff'd, 272 F.3d 333 F.3d (6th Cir. 2001).

Several tax court cases follow *Gross*, the most recent being *Gallagher*,[10] which also held S corp income was not to be tax affected because the taxpayer's expert did not explain his reasons for tax affecting the earnings for valuation purposes, and, absent an argument to do so, the court declined to tax affect the earnings.[11]

Can the expert explain the reason for the tax rate he or she used to tax affect the income to capitalize?

Gross and its progeny are tax court cases. The tax courts address estate and gift tax issues. Two fair value cases, a Delaware dissenter's rights case (*Delaware Open MRI*[12]) and a Massachusetts family law case (*Bernier*[13]) approach tax affecting differently. Whereas *Gross* held that the appropriate tax rate was 0%, *Delaware Open MRI* created a formula that accounted for the benefit S corp shareholders receive by avoiding the double taxation of C corp income. As explained above, this occurs because the C corporation pays taxes on the income it reports. Then, when the C corporation pays a dividend to the stockholder, he or she reports the income and pays income tax on the dividend. Thus, the income is taxed twice: first, by the corporation, when it is reported, and, second, by the shareholder, when he or she receives a dividend. On the other hand, the S corporation does not pay taxes on the income it reports; the individual shareholders report the income on their personal tax return and pay any taxes due. If the S corp then distributes this previously taxed income, it is not taxable to the stockholders. Thus, the income is taxed once. The *Delaware Open MRI* formula attempts to calculate this tax benefit. In the *Delaware Open MRI* case, the formula reduced the taxes from 40% corporate tax rate to approximately 29.4%. This formula did not account for state income taxes.

Most experts use either the actual individual or corporate tax rate (if they believe the most logical buyer would be a C corporation or they do not believe there is a benefit to S corp status) or a reduced tax rate to express the "premium" or "valued added" of a pass-through entity due to no double taxation to an S corp shareholder. Another method that is gaining prominence is to quantify the "premium" or "value added" by using personal tax rates and adjusting the discount rate slightly downward thereby increasing the value.

10 *Estate of Louise Paxton Gallagher, et al., Petitioner v. Commissioner of the Internal Revenue Service*, Respondent, T. C. Memo 2011-148.

11 Note that these cases are called memo decisions by the U.S. Tax Court and presumably only applicable to the case at hand.

12 *Del. Open MRI Radiology Assocs., P.A. v. Kessler*, 898 A.2d 290, 2006 Del. Ch. LEXIS 84, 2006 WL 4764042 (Del. Ch. 2006).

13 *Bernier v. Bernier*, 449 Mass. 774, 873 N.E.2d 216, 2007 Mass. LEXIS 598 (Mass. 2007).

In any event, the expert should be able to carefully explain the reasoning behind which method he or she uses in tax affecting an S corp or other types of pass-through entities.

CASE STUDY: TAX AFFECTING

Let us return to our case study and the income to capitalize chosen by Expert No. 1 and No. 2. To this point, the experts have normalized the company's income and chosen the income before taxes to capitalize. We now address tax affecting the income to capitalize. In this example, Expert No. 1 uses the actual marginal tax rate of the company and Expert No. 2 reduces the tax rate because of the "pass-through" benefits of an S corp. Assume the actual tax rate on Expert No. 1's $180,000 is 35% ($63,000) and the "reduced" tax rate on Expert No. 2's $300,000 is 25% ($75,000).[14]

Using the same 20% cap rate we have been using in this case study, Expert No. 1's value would be $585,000 and Expert No. 2's would be $1,125,000 as follows:

	Expert No. 1	Expert No. 2
Pre-tax income to capitalize	$180,000	$300,000
Taxes	(63,000)	(75,000)
After tax income to capitalize	117,000	225,000
Divided by	20%	20%
Value	$585,000	$1,125,000

The following chart presents the after-tax income to capitalize of each expert and includes a column for the judge to calculate his or her tax rate.

14 In this instance, the expert who valued the PTE uses some version of *Delaware MRI*, arriving at 25%. Other methods can be used. See Nancy J. Fannon and Keith Sellers, *Taxes and Value: The Ongoing Research and Analysis Relating to the S Corporation Valuation Puzzle*, Business Valuation Resources, 2015. Available at www.bvresources.com/publications.

INCOME TO CAPITALIZE COMPARISON

	Year	Expert No. 1	Expert No. 2	Judge
	1	$200,000	$300,000	
	2	180,000		
	3	160,000		
	4	175,000		
	5	150,000		
		2,700,000		
Divided by		15		
Pre tax income to capitalize		$180,000	$300,000	
Taxes		(63,000)	(75,000)	
After tax income to capitalize		$117,000	$225,000	
Other (i.e., projection)				

See Appendix 3 for a blank comparison chart that can be used to compare the experts' income to capitalize.

QUESTIONS TO ASK

1. Why does the expert believe his or her determination of the normalized income to capitalize best represents the expected future performance of the company?
2. Why would a business that has been shrinking suddenly grow?
3. If the expert includes income from five years ago, why is it relevant?
4. Can the expert explain the reason for the tax rate used to tax affect the income to capitalize?

In the next section, we examine the critical components of the cap rate (discount rate less growth rate) and the questions to ask to evaluate each expert's computation of the cap rate.

CAPITALIZATION RATE[15]

POINTS COVERED IN THIS SECTION

- The discount rate minus the long-term growth rate is known as the capitalization rate; and
- Two critical components in the cap rate are risk (R) and growth (G).

The discount rate minus the average long-term growth rate is known as the capitalization rate. It can be expressed as a percentage when it is used as a divisor (i.e., 20%) or as a number when it is used as a multiple (i.e., 5). A cap rate is the inverse of a multiplier. A cap rate of 20%, or 0.20, is the same as a multiplier of 5; a cap rate of 33%, or 0.333, is the same as a multiplier of 3. You multiply the income to capitalize by a multiplier; you divide the adjusted earnings by a cap rate.

$$\$117,000 \div 0.20 = \$585,000$$
$$\$117,000 \times 5 = \$585,000$$

The cap rate equals the discount rate less the long-term growth rate. If we assume a discount rate of 0.23 (23%) and a long-term growth rate of 0.03 (3%) for our cap rate of 0.20, the formula would look like this:

Discount rate	0.23
Less: Long-term growth	(0.03)
Cap rate	0.20

The determination of the discount rate and the average long-term growth rate each involve analysis and judgment on the part of the expert. One way to test the opinion is to have the experts explain how they differ and why their cap rate is correct.

Have the experts explain how they differ and why their cap rate is correct.

15 A capitalization rate is the rate used to convert income or cash flows into value.

Discount Rate

POINTS COVERED IN THIS SECTION

- Think of a discount rate in terms of an interest rate. Converting a future income stream to its present worth is the opposite of compounding, meaning, because you have to wait for the money and lose the opportunity to invest it and get interest, a dollar a year from now is not worth a dollar today.
- Generally, two methodologies are used to calculate a discount rate:
  - Capital asset pricing model (CAPM); and
  - Buildup method.
- These methods begin with risk-free rate (typically the 20-year Treasury bonds), which is then increased to account for the fact that stocks are riskier than bonds, especially ownership interests in closely held businesses.

Risk. The discount rate is the first component of the capitalization rate. It is a function of the certainty of achieving the predicted future results. That is the essence of risk. We have said that value is the present worth of future benefits. This underlying premise is part of all valuation approaches but can be seen most clearly in the income approach.

Value is future-oriented, and the future is uncertain. *Therefore, the more uncertain a company's future prospects are, the riskier the company will be and the higher the discount rate will be. If expressed in terms of a multiple, the riskier the company, the lower the multiple will be.* Elements of risk can be a function of past performance, size, and market factors. A buyer wants to pay less for a riskier company. That is because, in a risky business, a purchaser wants to get its purchase price back sooner. If the business is stable or growing, the buyer will wait longer. A sanity test is to compare a multiplier to the number of years the buyer will wait to recoup his or her purchase price. Depending on the facts, the purchaser will wait five years for a healthy business, more for a growing business, and two and a half years for a risky business. The more risky the company, the higher the discount rate will be. The higher the discount rate, the lower the value of the company will be. In essence, as the risk increases, the discount rate increases. Thus, discount rates are higher and values are lower for riskier companies.

↑ Risk

↑ Discount rate

↓ Value

One should think of a discount rate in terms of an interest rate forgone because you are waiting for your money. Converting a future income stream to its present worth is the opposite of compounding. So, if you put $100 in the bank for a year and get interest at 5%, at the end of the year, you would have $105. Conversely, if you waited a year to get your $100, you wouldn't pay that much ($100) because you would lose a year's worth of interest. In this example, you would pay $95 to get $100 in a year at 5%. So the present worth of $100 a year from now is $95.[16]

The court should pay particular attention to how the expert arrives at the discount rate. Generally, experts calculate the discount rate using two methodologies that are very similar. These are the capital asset pricing model, commonly referred to as CAPM,[17] and the buildup method. Following is the theory for these two methods.

Risk is nothing more than uncertainty as to receiving money in the future: The more certain you are about receiving your money, the less risk you are taking on. Likewise, an investor will pay less for a more risky asset and more for a less risky asset. Therefore, Treasury bills and municipal bonds, which are backed by the U.S. government, are considered less risky and pay lower interest rates than corporate bonds (which are not backed by the U.S. government). Stocks are considered more risky than corporate bonds and demand a higher return than corporate bonds. Corporate bonds can be secured, but even unsecured bondholders are paid before the shareholders (owners) are paid. If the economy is in turmoil, this is even more evident. In today's environment, money market funds, certificates of deposit, and Treasury bills pay almost no interest because they have very little risk and they mature in a short period. Corporate bonds demand a higher interest rate, and stocks demand even higher returns because they have a longer time to repayment and there is a risk they won't be repaid.

16 Using a discount rate of 5%

17 This is referred to as cap (like a baseball cap) and the letter M, said separately: Cap M.

As of June 30, 2016, these rates were:[18]

Instrument	June 30, 2016
Treasury bills (secondary market)	
4-week	0.19%
3-month	0.26%
6-month	0.35%
1-year	0.44%
Treasury constant maturities	
6-month	0.36%
1-year	0.45%
5-year	1.01%
10-year	1.49%
20-year	1.86%
Corporate bonds	
Aaa	3.39%
Baa	4.41%

As you can see by comparing the yields on U.S. Treasury bills with Aaa/Baa corporate bonds, more risky investments demand higher returns. The expert should explain all of the risks associated with the company being valued. These risks include the risks of the economy as a whole, the risks of the particular industry, and the risks of the particular company. The CAPM and the buildup methods calculate the returns demanded by starting with a risk-free 20-year U.S. Treasury bond and increasing the required rate of return for the added risk of stocks as a whole, smaller stocks, the particular industry, and the particular company. These components are called the risk-free rate, the equity risk premium, industry risk, the size premium, and specific company risk. Using the 23% discount rate we have discussed, the formula for the buildup method looks like this as of June 30, 2016:

Risk-free rate	1.86
+ Equity risk premium	6.03
± Industry risk	–
+ Size premium	5.60
± Specific company risk	9.50
= Discount rate	**0.23**

18 Federal Reserve Statistical Release, July 5, 2016.

The following is a description of each of these elements of the discount rate with the judgments the expert will make and the questions they should be asked.

Risk-free rate. This is the 20-year Treasury bond rate as of the valuation date. There is no judgment; the expert looks up this number on a chart.

Equity risk premium (ERP). This is the rate of return added to the risk-free rate to reflect additional risks of large-company stocks (i.e., S&P 500) over a risk-free, government-backed 20-year Treasury bond. The ERP is derived from the *Valuation Handbook - U.S. Guide to Cost of Capital,*[19] which is compiled by Duff & Phelps. Duff & Phelps publishes historical ERPs from multiple periods. This premium is the average annual amount that returns for stocks have exceeded returns on the 20-year Treasury bond rate over this period. Using the above numbers, so far the rate of return is 8.89 (1.86 + 6.03).

Industry risk premium. This can increase or decrease the rate of return and, therefore, change the conclusion of value significantly. This premium adjustment measures whether the industry in which the company operates is more or less risky than the market as a whole. The expert needs to clearly identify that the companies in the grouping are comparable to the subject company and that there are enough comparable companies. There is also controversy concerning the use of the industry premium. Some experts do not use the industry premium due to the issue of comparable companies and other factors. When the expert uses this premium, he or she will typically need to answer technical questions under cross-examination to convince the court that there is a valid basis for this adjustment and that it makes sense.

Size premium. The size premium increases the rate of return when the subject company is smaller than the average size of a publicly traded company. There are various sources where this information can be found.

> Because of the amount of discretion in this adjustment, it should be thoroughly questioned.

Specific company risk premium. The largest amount of discretion occurs in the expert's choice of the specific company risk premium. The expert determines how risky the subject company is. Typical areas that affect the risk of a business are the depth of management, competition, customer concentration, product lines, geographic locations, debt, shrinking or expanding profit margins, etc. This adjustment is based on the expert's judgment. As such, it is typically the largest area of disagreement, if not the only area of disagreement, between the experts.

19 *The Valuation Handbook - U.S. Guide to Cost of Capital* is available at www.bvresources.com/publications.

QUESTIONS TO ASK

1. Has the expert chosen the appropriate Treasury bond rate, equity risk premium, industry risk premium, and size premium?
2. Has the expert determined the appropriate specific company risk premium?

Growth Rate

POINTS COVERED IN THIS SECTION

- This rate is the company's average long-term sustainable growth rate; and
- The growth rate can dramatically affect value because it increases both income and the cap rate.

Growth is the second component that is used to build a capitalization rate. Once the expert determines the income to capitalize and the discount rate, he or she needs to select the rate at which the income will grow over the long term, not just for the next year. The growth rate used should be the company's average long-term sustainable growth rate. This computation requires judgment. Usually, income is expected to grow consistently, at least, with the rate of inflation. This should not be a large number, such as 15%. To provide context, the Livingston Survey, published by the Philadelphia Federal Reserve, issues forecasts of 10-year inflation. According to the September 2012 Livingston Survey, median 10-year inflation is forecast to be 2.5%. The income may grow somewhat faster if the industry within which the business operates is growing at a faster rate. Therefore, long-term growth rates generally range from 0% to 5%.

QUESTION TO ASK:

1. Has the expert chosen the appropriate long-term growth rate in light of past performance, expected future performance, and the economic and industry conditions?

Operation of Cap Rate

POINTS COVERED IN THIS SECTION

- Even small changes to the discount rate or the growth rate can have a large effect on value.

As discussed earlier, the formula for the computation of the cap rate is:

$$\text{Discount rate (R) - Growth (G) = Cap rate}$$

The full formula for the computation of value is:

$$\frac{(\text{Income})\ (1 + G)}{R - G}$$

or

$$\frac{(\text{Income})\ (1 + G)}{\text{Cap rate}}$$

GROWTH RATES

The growth rate can dramatically affect value because it increases future income and decreases the cap rate (the lower the cap rate, the higher the multiple). Using growth rates of 2%, 4%, and 6% in our case study has the following results for the after-tax income to capitalize of $117,000 for Expert No. 1 and $225,000 for Expert No. 2.

For Expert No. 1—$117,000:

2% Growth Rate	4% Growth Rate	6% Growth Rate
$\frac{(117{,}000)\ (1.02)}{0.23 - 0.02}$	$\frac{(117{,}000)\ (1.04)}{0.23 - 0.04}$	$\frac{(117{,}000)\ (1.06)}{(0.23 - 0.06)}$
$\frac{119{,}340}{0.21}$	$\frac{121{,}680}{0.19}$	$\frac{124{,}000}{0.17}$
$568,300	$640,400	$729,500

For Expert No. 2—$225,000:

2% Growth Rate	4% Growth Rate	6% Growth Rate
$\frac{(225{,}000)\ (1.02)}{0.23 - 0.02}$	$\frac{(225{,}000)\ (1.04)}{0.23 - 0.04}$	$\frac{(225{,}000)\ (1.06)}{0.23 - 0.06}$
$\frac{229{,}500}{0.21}$	$\frac{234{,}000}{0.19}$	$\frac{238{,}500}{0.17}$
$1,092,900	$1,231,600	$1,402,900

Thus, where the after-tax income is $117,000 or $225,000, the discount rate is 23% and the growth rates are 2%, 4%, or 6%, the value ranges from $568,300 to $1,402,900.

Discount rate: 23%

	Income to Capitalize	
Growth %	**$117,000**	**$225,000**
2	$568,300	$1,092,900
4	$640,400	$1,231,600
6	$729,500	$1,402,900

Here, the range of value goes from $568,300 to $1,402,900, approximately an $800,000 difference, and we have not yet addressed the discount rate.

Experts often disagree on the discount rate as well. Remember, the discount rate expresses risk. Increasing the discount rate lowers value because, when risk goes up, value goes down.

Risk ↑ Value ↓

Where risk decreases, value goes up.

Risk ↓ Value ↑

The interesting point is that, while these differences are dramatic, the individual judgments that lead to these differences in the determination of the income to capitalize and the cap rate can be small and seem logical. Therefore, it is important to understand how each of these judgments was reached and to place them in context. To illustrate this point, we return to our case study.

CASE STUDY: CAP RATE COMPARISON

In our case study, Expert No. 1 chooses a cap rate of 23%, consisting of a discount rate of 25% and a long-term growth rate of 2% (25% - 2% = 23%). Expert No. 2 chooses a cap rate of 15%, consisting of a discount rate of 21% and a long-term growth rate of 6% (21% - 6% = 15%). The comparison of their calculations is presented below with a column for the judge to make his or her determination of specific company risk and the long-term growth rate. (The risk-free rate and the equity risk premium are objective numbers and should be the same for both experts.)

CAP RATE COMPARISON			
	Expert No. 1	**Expert No. 2**	**Judge**
Risk-free rate	0.04	0.04	0.04
+ Equity risk	0.07	0.07	0.07
± Industry risk	0.01	-	
+ Size premium	0.03	0.03	0.03
Specific company risk	0.10	0.07	
Discount rate	0.25	0.21	
Less: growth rate	(0.02)	0.06	
Cap rate	23	15	

If we use Expert No. 1's after-tax income to capitalize of $117,000 and his or her cap rate of 23%, the value equals $518,900.

$$\frac{(117{,}000)\ (1.02)}{0.25 - 0.02}$$

$$\frac{119{,}340}{0.23}$$

= $518,900

Similarly, if we use Expert No. 2's after-tax income to capitalize of $225,000 and cap rate of 15%, the value equals $1,590,000.

$$\frac{(225{,}000)\ (1.06)}{0.21 - 0.06}$$

$$\frac{238{,}500}{0.15}$$

= $1,590,000

The range in values is now $518,900 to $1,590,000.

See Appendix 4 for a blank cap rate comparison chart that can be used to compare the experts' cap rates.

QUESTION TO ASK:

1. Which expert has best explained and documented his or her choice of a specific company risk premium and a long-term growth rate?

Summary

In the income capitalization method, the expert does the following:

1. Makes adjustments to income
   a. Compare the adjustments
   b. Do the adjustments make sense?
2. Determines income to capitalize
   a. Compare reasons
3. Determines the tax effect on the income
   a. Compare reasons
4. Determines the cap rate
   a. Discount rate
      i. Compare reasons
   b. Long-term growth rate
      i. Compare reasons

We now move to the discounted cash flow method.

Discounted Cash Flow Method

POINTS COVERED IN THIS SECTION

- The discounted cash flow (DCF) method is used when the expected future earnings cannot be represented by a single period as in the capitalization of earnings method because they are expected to change;
- DCF calculations may appear very complicated, depending on the level of detail used (and available) for revenue and expense projections, but there are certain critical components:
  - Normalized earnings;
  - Projected revenues;
  - Projected expenses;
  - Tax affect;
  - Discount rate; and
  - Terminal value.
- The discount rate is the cap rate without the growth rate;
- The expert will:
  - Normalize earnings as in the capitalization of earnings method;
  - Determine the discount rate in the same manner as the income capitalization method; and
  - Then, instead of determining the long-term growth rate, the expert projects the expected revenue and expenses over several years and then determines a terminal value when the business has stabilized and applies a long-term growth rate.
- Typically, this methodology will produce a different value than the one arrived at by the capitalization of earnings method; and
- With computer programs, the complex formulas in the DCF are easy to apply, but these formulas also have critical components that must be examined.

The discounted cash flow (DCF) method is used when a single period cannot represent the expected future earnings. Most often, this occurs when the income in the immediate future is expected to be different from the income in the past and in the long-term future. For instance, if sales are expected to increase dramatically for the next few years and then remain relatively constant because of the introduction of a new product, an expert would use this method. In essence, the relevant factors that affect the sales and expenses must be considered and analyzed in order to determine the expected future earnings. In this methodology, the expert or (if possible) company management will project the expected future revenues and expenses. The expert will use a discount rate to "discount" the income back to present value (because dollars received in the future are worth less than dollars received today). This can be the same discount rate used in the capitalization of income method, computed using the buildup method or the CAPM method.

The discount rate is the cap rate without the growth rate:

Discount rate: 23%
Growth: N/A
Cap rate: N/A

DCF Calculations

DCF calculations may appear very complicated, depending on the level of detail used (and available) for revenue and expense projections. These models are based upon projected cash flow, not income. However, for simplicity in our examples, we have used net income. Below, we continue our case study with Expert No. 1 and Expert No. 2's DCF calculations. We begin with normalized earnings, as presented by each expert in the capitalization of earnings section. Each expert grows revenues and expenses at the rates they deem appropriate until they believe the earnings of the company have stabilized. The experts should have detailed explanations to support their estimates of growth and/or decline for the company's projected revenues, expenses, and tax affect.

Once the experts use DCF projections, they apply a present value factor to the after-tax net income of each projected year, based upon the selected discount rate.[20]

Terminal Value

Once earnings are stabilized (i.e., no dramatic increases or decreases are expected within revenues or expenses), the expert calculates a value for the terminal year. The terminal-year earnings equal the estimated future long-term earnings of the company just like the earnings in the capitalized earnings method. The terminal-year earnings are then capitalized under the same formula as the capitalization of earnings method. The result is the value of the projected future income as of the last projected year (Year 4 in this example). This value is, therefore, discounted using the same present value factor as in the last projected year.

20 For our examples, we have used the end-of-year convention to calculate the present value factors versus using the midyear convention. Midyear discounting is appropriate when cash flows are received throughout the year. For example, when the owners take periodic bonuses and do not wait to the end of the year. End-of-year discounting assumes all cash flows are received at the end of the year.

The final step is to add the present valued figures. This total equals the value of the company as of the valuation date.

CASE STUDY: DISCOUNTED CASH FLOW

In the capitalization of earnings method, Expert No. 1 produced a value of $518,900 and Expert No. 2 produced a value of $1,590,000, a difference of $1,071,100. Under the DCF method, Expert No. 1 produced a value of $412,000 and Expert No. 2 produced a value of $1,726,000, a difference of $1,314,000. This difference arose because the first expert began with lower normalized earnings. He or she then increased revenues at a lesser rate and expenses at a greater rate and chose a higher discount rate. Expert No. 1 tax affected the income at 35%, and Expert No. 2 tax affected the income at 25%.

When we compare the computation of the present value of Year 1 of the projection for Experts No. 1 and No. 2, we begin to see how this large discrepancy is created.

	Year 1		
	Expert		
Increase %	**No. 1**	**No. 2**	
Sales	8%	12%	
Cost of sales	8%	12%	
Operating expenses	8%	12%	
Discount rate	25%	20%	
Tax rate	35%	25%	
Amount			
Sales	$1,890,000	$1,982,400	
<Cost of sales>	(923,400)	(935,200)	
Gross profit	966,600	1,047,200	
<Operating expenses>	(750,600)	(711,200)	
Pretax income	216,000	336,000	
Taxes	(75,600)	(84,000)	
After-tax income	140,400	252,000	
Present value factor	0.800	0.833	Difference
Present value	$112,320	$210,000	$97,680

Thus, after one year, we have a difference of $97,680, which grows each year because of the different judgments on the critical components made by Expert No. 1 and No. 2.

Expert No. 1

The full DCF valuation of Expert No. 1 is set forth below.

Increase	Current	Year 1	Year 2	Year 3	Year 4	Terminal Year
Sales (2)		8%	6%	4%	3%	3%
Cost of sales (3)		8%	8%	8%	4%	
Operating expenses (3)		8%	8%	8%	4%	
Discount rate	25%					
Amount						
Sales	$1,750,000	$1,890,000	$2,003,400	$2,083,536	$2,146,042	
<Cost of goods>	(855,000)	(923,400)	(997,272)	(1,077,054)	(1,120,136)	(Term Year) (1 + G) / R - G
Gross profit	895,000	966,600	1,006,128	1,006,482	1,025,906	
<Operating expenses>	(695,000)	(750,600)	(810,648)	(875,500)	(910,520)	
Pretax income (1)	200,000	216,000	195,480	130,982	115,386	
Taxes @ 35% (4)		(75,600)	(68,418)	(45,844)	(40,385)	
After-tax income		140,400	127,062	85,138	75,001	
Terminal value (5)		-	-	-	-	(75,001) (1.03) / 0.25 - 0.03 = $351,141
Present value factor (6)		0.800	0.640	0.512	0.410	0.410
Present value		$112,320	$81,320	$43,591	$30,720	$143,827
Value						$411,778
Rounded						$412,000

Expert No. 1 assumes the following:

1. Pretax income is normalized at $200,000 as in the capitalization of earnings method.
2. Sales will grow at rates of 8%, 6%, 4%, and 3% for Years 1 through 4, respectively.
3. Cost of sales and operating expenses increase at 8%, 8%, 8%, and 4%.
4. The tax rate is 35%.
5. The discount rate equals 25%. Terminal-year long-term growth equals 3%.
6. A discount rate of 25% equates to the present value set forth above.

The above assumptions produce a value of $412,000 (rounded) as set forth in the chart above.

Expert No. 2

The full valuation of Expert No. 2 is set forth below.

Increase	Current	Year 1	Year 2	Year 3	Year 4	Terminal Year	
Sales (2)		12%	10%	10%	4%	4%	
Cost of sales (3)		12%	10%	10%	4%		
Operating expenses (3)		12%	10%	10%	4%		
Discount rate	20%						
Amount							
Sales	$1,770,000	$1,982,400	$2,180,640	$2,398,704	$2,494,652		
<Cost of goods>	(835,000)	(935,200)	(1,028,720)	(1,131,592)	(1,176,856)	(Term Year) (1 + G) / R - G	
Gross profit	935,000	1,047,200	1,151,920	1,267,112	1,317,796		
<Operating expenses>	(635,000)	(711,200)	(782,320)	(860,552)	(894,974)		
Pretax income (1)	300,000	336,000	369,600	406,560	422,822		
Taxes @ 25% (4)		(84,000)	(92,400)	(101,640)	(105,706)		
After-tax income		252,000	277,200	304,920	317,117		
Terminal value (5)		-	-	-	-	(317,117) (1.04) / 0.20-0.04	= 2,061,261
Present value factor (6)		0.833	0.694	0.579	0.482	0.482	
Present value		$210,000	$192,500	$176,458	$152,930	$994,049	
Value						$1,725,938	
Rounded						$1,726,000	

Expert No. 2 assumes the following:

1. Pretax income is normalized at $300,000 as in the capitalization of earnings method.
2. Sales will grow at rates of 12%, 10%, 10%, and 4% for Years 1 through 4, respectively.
3. Cost of sales and operating expenses remain constant as a percentage of sales.
4. The tax rate is 25%
5. The discount rate equals 20%. Terminal-year long-term growth equals 4%.
6. A discount rate of 20% equates to the present value factors set forth above.

The above assumptions produce a value of $1,726,000 as set forth in the chart above.

The biggest issues with this method are to grow revenues at the appropriate rate and to properly match revenues and expenses needed to achieve this growth. If expenses are too high and increase at too great a rate, the value will be too low. On the other hand, the value will be overstated if the expert grows revenue without accounting for the necessary expenses. For example, if the expert does not include the requirement for a new factory to produce the product because there is not enough capacity at the current facility, the value will be overstated. The expert will need to explain the different factors he or she took into consideration in order to arrive at his or her cash flow.

The following is a comparison of their positions with a column for the judge to make his or her determination. This chart can be used to compare percentages and actual amounts.

DISCOUNTED CASH FLOW COMPARISON							
	Year	Expert #1		Expert #2		Judge	
		Amount	%	Amount	%	Amount	%
Normalized pretax income		$200,000		$300,000			
Sales							
(% growth)	1	1,890,000	8	1,982,400	12		
	2	2,003,400	6	2,180,640	10		
	3	2,083,536	4	2,398,704	10		
	4	2,146,042	3	2,494,652	4		
Cost of sales							
(% growth)							
	1	923,400	8	935,200	12		
	2	997,272	8	1,028,720	10		
	3	1,077,054	8	1,131,592	10		
	4	1,120,136	4	1,176,856	4		
Operating expenses							
(% growth)							
	1	750,600	8	711,200	12		
	2	810,648	8	782,320	10		
	3	875,500	8	860,552	10		
	4	910,520	4	894,974	4		
Tax rate			35		25		
Discount rate			25		20		
Terminal value		$351,141		$2,061,261			
Discount rate			25		20		
Less: long-term growth			3		4		
Cap rate			22		16		

See Appendix 5 for a blank discounted cash flow comparison chart that can be used to compare the experts' excess earnings computations.

QUESTIONS TO ASK

1. Why do you believe the (multiperiod) DCF method is more appropriate than the (single-period) capitalization of earnings method?

Revenues:

1. Can revenues realistically grow at the projected rates?

Expenses:

1. Do the expenses support the revenues? For example:

   a. Are there enough employees?

   b. Does an additional factory need to be built to produce the product?

Discount rate:

1. Does the discount rate adequately present the risk of achieving the projection?

Terminal value:

1. Is the long-term growth rate used in the terminal value calculation adequately explained?

Chapter 4. Asset-Based Approach

POINTS COVERED IN THIS CHAPTER

- The expert considers the assets and liabilities of the company.
- This method is typically used in valuing entities that either hold assets such as real estate entities and/or other types of tangible (hard) asset intensive businesses, such as timber or mining companies.
- Two basic methods under the asset approach:
  - Net asset value method
    Used for holding entities (entities that merely hold assets) or asset-intensive companies that are expected to continue in business.
  - Liquidation value method
    Considered when the income generated by the company is insufficient to sustain it.

As mentioned previously, value is defined as the present worth of the expected future benefits. It is easy to see how this works with the income approach but less obvious when considering the asset approach. In this approach, the expert considers the assets and liabilities of the company that are listed on the company's balance sheet at their accounting value,[1] which is not necessarily their economic or fair market value.

There are also assets and liabilities that may not be listed on the balance sheet that should be considered. Examples include intangible assets such as goodwill and liabilities such as environmental liabilities.

1 The accounting values you will most often see are the cost of the asset or liability reduced for depreciation on real estate and fixed assets

There are two basic methods under the asset-based approach: the net asset value method and the liquidation value method. Both of these methods replace the assets and liabilities listed at their accounting values with their economic values. The difference between the methods is the time and cost needed to dispose of the assets and extinguish the liabilities. In the net asset value method, a longer time is contemplated, as well as the sufficiency of income, to justify the asset values. In the liquidation value method, there is less time contemplated for disposal of the assets. Liquidation value can be orderly or forced.

Most experts believe that the asset-based approach should be used only when valuing a controlling interest in a business. However, adjustments can be made to allow its use in the valuation of minority interests.

> In the valuation of real estate entities, business valuation experts will rely on real estate appraisers. Most likely, the biggest difference in the experts' conclusions of value will be between the real estate appraisers' values for the real estate.

The following is a simplified version of the net asset value method for a real estate holding entity, which is the type of valuations the court is most likely to see. The most important adjustment is to bring the real estate to market value from accounting value.

			Adjustment	Adjusted Balance Sheet
Cash	$20,000			$20,000
Receivable	-	(a)	$10,000	10,000
Property	700,000	(b)	1,300,000	2,000,000
Depreciation	(200,000)	(b)	200,000	-
Total assets	520,000			2,030,000
Accounts payable	-	(c)	15,000	15,000
Mortgage	200,000			200,000
Equity	320,000	(d)	$1,495,000	1,815,000
Total liability and equity	$520,000			$2,030,000

(a) To record receivable of $10,000.
(b) To record land at appraised value of $2,000,000 and remove depreciation.
(c) To record accounts payables of $15,000.
(d) To record the net change to equity.

The net asset value method is used for asset holding entities and/or asset-intensive companies that are expected to continue in business. The liquidation method is considered when the income the company generated is insufficient to sustain it. It would be the method used to value the retail store in our case study or any other entity that was going out of business. Therefore, normally it would not be appropriate for a profitable real estate holding company as presented above. The liquidation methodology accounts for the costs of liquidation, the write-downs necessary to dispose of the assets or pay off the liabilities, and the time value of money (present value) for the period needed to complete the liquidation.

The liquidation method is not often encountered in matrimonial matters. However, if the business does not generate enough income to justify its existence, i.e., it is worth more dead than alive, the liquidation method may be the appropriate valuation method. This method is usually only considered when a liquidation is contemplated or is about to occur.

The following is a simplified example of the liquidation method for a retail store that does *not* own real estate:

			Adjustment	Adjusted Balance Sheet
Cash	$20,000	(a)	($15,000)	$5,000
Accounts receivable	200,000	(b)	(80,000)	120,000
Inventory	500,000	(c)	(250,000)	250,000
Furniture and fixtures	600,000	(d)	(450,000)	150,000
Accumulated depreciation	(300,000)		300,000	-
Total assets	1,020,000			525,000
Accounts payable	100,000			100,000
Loans	200,000			200,000
Equity	720,000	(e)	($495,000)	225,000
Total liabilities and equity	$1,020,000			$525,000

(a) To record the costs of liquidation.
(b) To record receivables at $0.60 on the $1.
(c) To write down inventory to $0.50 on the $1.
(d) To record furniture and fixtures at $0.25 on the $1 and remove depreciation.
(e) To record the net change to equity.

The net asset value method will be the methodology the court most often sees in the asset approach. Furthermore, this will most likely be the method for a real estate holding company. Accordingly, this case study deals with a real estate holding company.

CASE STUDY: REAL ESTATE HOLDING COMPANY

Net Asset Value Method

In the following example, the company has cash, a note receivable, rent receivables, real estate, a mortgage, and accounts payable. Both experts agree on the amount of cash, rent receivable, and the mortgage balance.

Expert No. 1 opines that the note receivable is not collectible and accounts payable equal $50,000. He or she relies on a real estate appraiser who values the building at $2,000,000. Expert No. 2 opines that the note of $30,000 is collectible, the accounts payable equal $20,000, and relies on a real estate appraiser who values the building at $2,500,000. The following is a comparison on their positions with a column for the judge to make a determination on the disputed positions.

NET ASSETS COMPARISON

	Expert No. 1	Expert No. 2	Judge
Assets			
Cash	$5,000	$5,000	$5,000
Rent receivable	10,000	10,000	10,000
Note	-	30,000	
Building	2,000,000	2,500,000	
Liabilities			
Accounts payable	(50,000)	(20,000)	
Mortgage	(1,000,000)	(1,000,000)	(1,000,000)
Net equity	$965,000	$1,525,000	

To determine the net equity of this entity, the court will need to make findings on the values of the building, the collectability of the note, and the amount of accounts payable.

See Appendix 6 for a blank net assets comparison chart that can be used to compare the experts' net assets computations.

QUESTIONS TO ASK:

1. Is this an asset-holding entity or an asset-intensive business such as real estate, which is appropriate for the methodology?
2. Have the experts accounted for all the assets and liabilities?
3. Do the experts differ because of different real property valuations?

Chapter 5. Hybrid-Excess Earnings Method

POINTS COVERED IN THIS CHAPTER

- Considers benefits derived from both income and assets.
- Not particularly useful in valuing high-growth companies.
- The author of the method, the IRS, cautions its use to when there is no better method.
- It is used most often to value small businesses and professional practices. As such, experts in matrimonial matters frequently use it.
- Value is computed as follows:
    - Net tangible assets + goodwill = total value of the equity of the business (stock)
- Procedures:
    1. Determine the fair market value of net tangible assets.
    2. Determine the rate of return on the net tangible assets.
    3. Normalize earnings and determine the income to capitalize as in the capitalization of earnings method. The expert makes a series of judgments that can greatly affect value.
    4. Calculate the excess earnings as income to capitalize less the rate of return on net tangible assets.
    5. Determine the cap rate on excess earnings.
    6. Calculate goodwill by capitalizing the excess earnings.
    7. Calculate the value of the business by adding the net tangible assets and the goodwill.

We call the excess earnings method a hybrid approach, as it considers benefits derived from both income and assets. This method was first used in the 1920s to compensate owners for the loss of their brewery and other alcohol-related businesses due to Prohibition. It is not particularly useful in valuing high-growth companies. The author of the method, the IRS, cautions its use to when there is no better method. The excess earnings method is used most often to value small businesses and professional practices. As such, experts in matrimonial matters frequently use it.

This method requires the expert to determine two rates of return: a return on the net tangible assets and a capitalization rate on the excess income. In essence, the expert determines a value for the net tangible assets and calculates a separate value for goodwill[1] using these two rates of return. Since capitalized excess earnings produce a value for goodwill that is added to the net tangible assets, the method is said to apply aspects of the asset approach and the income approach. Value is thus computed as follows:

Net tangible assets + Goodwill = Value

Procedures

The procedures used to determine the value under the excess earning method are:

1. Determine the fair market value of the net tangible assets, if practicable;
2. Determine the rate of return on the net tangible assets;
3. Normalize earnings and determine the income to capitalize as in the capitalization of earnings method;
4. Calculate the excess earnings as income to capitalize less the rate of return on net tangible assets;
5. Determine the cap rate applied to excess earnings;
6. Determine the goodwill based on the capitalization of excess earnings; and
7. Calculate the value of the business by adding the net tangible assets and the goodwill.

1 The excess earnings method is used to value goodwill, which is an unidentified intangible asset. Specifically identified intangibles, such as patents, would be valued separately under this method. However, patents, licenses, and other specifically identified intangibles are not typically addressed in the valuations of professional practices and small businesses valued under the excess earnings method. Therefore, for simplicity, they are not addressed here.

Determine the fair market value of the net tangible assets. First, if possible, the expert adjusts the assets and liabilities on the balance sheet to their fair market value. These adjustments are not always possible or practical; consequently, experts at times use book value. If adjustments are made, the net assets are calculated in the same method as in the net asset method of the asset approach as explained on page 58. In our example, we will assume that the company does not own any real estate, and the net tangible assets have a value of $240,000 after making the fair market adjustments.

Determine the rate of return on the net tangible assets. Second, after determining the value of the net tangible assets, the expert determines the appropriate rate of return for the net tangible assets. Think of this return as an interest rate. The rate of return on net assets is based on the risk associated with the assets. The more risky and illiquid the asset is, the higher the interest rate it requires. Ideally, the expert determines a rate of return on the individual categories of assets. Cash would require a money market rate. Accounts receivable, inventory, and equipment would require a rate a lender would require to loan against these assets. Equipment would require the rates that a bank would lend against them and so on. Any assets or portion of assets that a lender would not lend against would require an equity rate of return, which would equate to the returns calculated under the CAPM or buildup methods. This can become very complex; therefore, many experts use an average rate of return on all net assets. In our example, we use a single rate of return of 8% on the $240,000 of net tangible assets, which calculates a rate of return of $19,200.

Net assets:	$240,000
Rate of return:	8%
	$19,200

Normalize earnings and determine the income to capitalize as in the capitalization of earnings method. Third, the expert normalizes the income and determines the income to capitalize. All of the issues raised in the income approach come into play here. As in the income capitalization and discounted cash flow methods, the expert makes adjustments for:

1. Unreported income;
2. Personal expenses;
3. Nonrecurring income and expenses;

4. Extraordinary income and expenses;

5. Normalization adjustments;

6. Reasonable compensation; and

7. Tax affect.

Once again, the expert makes a series of judgments that can greatly affect value. After adjusting the earnings, the expert determines the income to capitalize by performing the same analysis as in the income capitalization method. In our example, we are assuming after-tax income to capitalize of $200,000.

Some experts capitalize pretax income. However, as previously stated, the expert should match the income to capitalize in the excess earnings to the cap rate. While it is not improper to use pretax income, it is difficult to derive from the market. As most rates are on an after-tax basis, the expert should choose a cap rate that expresses the risk associated with the income.

Calculate the excess earnings as income to capitalize less the return on net tangible assets. If the company's normalized earnings are above the return on net tangible assets, this excess is considered to be attributable to goodwill and other intangible assets. This rate of return will be subtracted from the income to capitalize to arrive at the excess earnings. Consequently, a higher rate of return produces less excess earnings and, therefore, lower goodwill. Conversely, a lower rate of return produces a higher amount of excess earnings and more goodwill. In our example, the excess earnings would equal $180,800:

After-tax income to capitalize	$200,000
Less: return on net tangible assets @ 8%	($19,200)
Excess earnings	$180,800

If the return on the tangible assets is greater than the income to capitalize, there is no goodwill under the excess earnings method. Using our example, the rate of return on net tangible assets is $19,200. Excess earnings of less than this amount would indicate that there was no goodwill. This would also call into question whether the company should be valued at less than the net tangible assets. In the event that the excess earnings are less than the return on net tangible assets, the expert should explain his or her conclusion of value and his or her reason for using this method.

Determine the cap rate on excess earnings and the goodwill based on the capitalization of excess earnings. In the income capitalization method, the capitalization rate capitalizes the entire income stream of the company in order to value the entire entity. The excess earnings being capitalized relate specifically to the income produced from the company's goodwill. The cap rate used under the excess earnings methodology must account for this difference. Most likely the excess earnings cap rate is higher than the cap rate used in the income capitalization method. In our example, we are using a cap rate of 24%.

Once the expert determines the excess earnings cap rate, goodwill is calculated based on the excess earnings the company generated as follows:

Excess earnings	$180,800
Divided by: capitalization rate	24%
Goodwill value	$753,333

Calculate the value of the business by adding the net tangible assets and the goodwill. The final step is to add the value of the net tangible assets and the goodwill to arrive at the value for the entire company. This is presented in a calculation similar to the one presented below.

Let us now combine all these elements and calculate the value of a company under the excess earnings method using the following assumptions:

1. The company's net tangible assets equal $240,000;
2. The rate of return equals 8%;
3. The after-tax income to capitalize equals $200,000; and
4. The capitalization rate equals 24%.

The calculation is as follows:

After-tax income to capitalize	$200,000
Less: return on net tangible assets at 8% (a)	(19,200)
Excess earnings	180,800
Divided by: capitalization rate	0.24
Goodwill value	753,333
Plus: net tangible assets	240,000
Company value	993,333
Rounded	$993,300

(a) $240,000 × 8% = $19,200

The excess earnings method contains critical components of net tangible assets, rate of return on net tangible assets, tax effects, income to capitalize, and a capitalization rate on excess earnings.

CASE STUDY: EXCESS EARNINGS METHOD

If the net tangible assets remain at $240,000 but the critical components of the rate of return on tangible assets, the income to capitalize, and the capitalization rate change by small amounts, the change in value can be dramatic. This can be seen if we use the income to capitalize from Expert No. 1 of $117,000 (a five-year weighted average) less taxes at 35% ($180,000 - $63,000 = $117,000) and Expert No. 2 of $225,000 (the normalized earnings of the final year) less taxes at 25% ($300,000 - $75,000 = $225,000). We then change the rate of return on tangible assets and the cap rate on the excess earnings by 2% lower or higher. If we use the income to capitalize of $117,000 from Expert No. 1 and increase both the rate of return on net tangible assets to 10% and increase the cap rate on excess earnings to 26%, the value of the business becomes $597,000. Using the income to capitalize of $225,000 from Expert No. 2, decreasing the rate of return on tangible assets from 8% to 6%, and lowering the capitalization rate to 22%, the value increases to $1,197,300.

The following is a chart that compares their positions with a column for the judge to make his or her determination of the disputed positions.

EXCESS EARNINGS COMPARISON						
		Expert No. 1		**Expert No. 2**		**Judge**
Income to capitalize		$117,000		$225,000		
Less rate of return on net tangible assets (a)	10%	24,000	6%	14,400	%	
Excess earnings		93,000		210,600		
Divided by: capitalization rate		26%		22%		
Goodwill value		357,700		957,300		
Plus: net tangible assets		240,000		240,000		
Company value		$597,700		$1,197,300		
Rounded						

(a) $240,000 × 10% = $24,000
$240,000 × 6% = $14,400

Thus the difference between the conclusions of the experts becomes $599,600 (1,197,300 - 597,700) after these changes.

See Appendix 7 for a blank excess earnings comparison chart, which can be used to compare the experts' excess earnings computations.

QUESTIONS TO ASK:

1. Which expert provided the best documentation and explanation for:
   a. Fair market value of net tangible assets (not always possible to do this; often use book value);
   b. Return on net tangible assets;
   c. Normalized earnings and income to capitalize;
   d. Excess earnings;
   e. Tax affects;
   f. Cap rate on excess earnings; and
   g. Goodwill.

Chapter 6. Market Approach

POINTS COVERED IN THIS CHAPTER

- The market approach calculates the value of a business or business interest being valued by comparison with actual transaction information.
- This information can be based on a transaction involving the entity itself, the value of shares of public companies (guideline public companies), or sales of entire companies (guideline transactions).
- Based on the principle of substitution—a prudent buyer will pay no more for a property than it would cost to acquire an equally desirable substitute.
- Two commonly used methods in the market approach are the "guideline public company method" and the "guideline transaction method."
- We focus on the guideline transaction method, more often seen in the valuation of smaller businesses.
- Use of this method has been facilitated, in recent years, by the development of databases including *Pratt's Stats*, BIZCOMPS, Done Deals, Institute of Business Experts (IBA), etc.
- The guideline transaction method is typically not relied upon exclusively and is often used as a check on the values the other methods indicate.

The market approach calculates value by comparing the business or business interest being valued by comparison with transaction information. This information can be based on transactions involving the entity itself, the value of guideline public companies, or guideline transactions. It is based on the principle of substitution, which states that a prudent buyer will pay no more for a property than it would cost to acquire an equally desirable substitute. Two commonly used methods in the market approach are the "guideline public company method" and the "guideline transaction method."

When using the market approach, the expert must be sure that the company being valued is similar to the selected public companies. The process is to identify "guideline" companies or transactions, analyze the similarities and differences, and develop multiples. The process of picking the guideline companies or transactions is done through the use of Standard Industrial Classification codes (SIC codes), North American Industry Classification System codes (NAICS codes), or business descriptions.

For small companies, you sometimes see multiples of gross revenue, i.e., 30%, 40%, and 50%. For revenues of $1,750,000, multiples of 30%, 40%, and 50% would produce the following values:

30%	40%	50%
$1,750,000	$1,750,000	$1,750,000
0.30	0.40	0.50
$525,000	$700,000	$875,000

Typically, these values do not include all the assets and liabilities of the company. Often the owner will keep his or her cash and receivables and pay his or her debts. The handling of inventory depends upon the data source used. The expert should address how he or she handles cash, receivables, inventory, and debt.

For larger companies, the multiples are typically applied to a measure of income or cash flow (net income), i.e., 4x, 5x, or 6x. Using the five-year weighted average of Expert No. 1, these multiples produce the following values:

$117,000	$117,000	$117,000
4x	5x	6x
$468,000	$585,000	$702,000

More often these values represent the value of the entire company, but again the expert should explain this. Let us now take a more detailed look at the guideline public company method.

Guideline public company method. We begin with the guideline public company method; however, *this method will only be seen in a small number of valuations because only a small number of public companies are sufficiently similar to many of the privately held companies being appraised to warrant a meaningful comparison.* For example, the local drugstore is usually not considered comparable to CVS and most coffee shops cannot be compared to Starbucks, etc. Further, except in the most unusual of circumstances, certain types of businesses have no publicly traded counterparts. These usually include medical practices, law firms, accounting firms, and many others. Essentially, the expert will pick public companies in the same or similar industry or with similar characteristics as the company being valued and learn about the public companies in order to determine those that may be comparable. He or she will then go through a process of comparison to see whether they are truly comparable.

First, the expert will compare the subject company to the guideline public company and ask questions such as: Is the guideline public company more diversified than the subject company? Does it sell the same products? Is it subject to the same economic influences? Are the companies mature or new? What markets do they serve?

Many experts do not use public companies as guideline companies if they are so large as not to be comparable to the subject company. The old "rule of thumb" was the public companies' revenues had to be within 10 times of the revenues of the subject company. However, what is important about size is the following: Is the guideline company more geographically diversified? Does it receive quantity discounts and other efficiencies? Does it have the same product line? How large is the company's capital pool (i.e., the company's access to money)? Other factors to consider are historical trends in growth and product prospects. Do the guideline public companies have significant research and development as compared to the subject company? The expert should also make comparisons to the financial and operating characteristics of the company.

Second, the expert will normalize the subject company's earnings (using the same process as discussed in the income approach) and then normalize the public companies' financial statements for items such as extraordinary items or nonrecurring items. Most public guideline companies are independently audited and, therefore, will not need generally accepted accounting principles (GAAP) and perquisite adjustments. The expert then uses the adjusted financial statements to prepare financial ratio analyses between the guideline companies and the subject company to help determine comparability between the subject company and the public companies. Through this analysis, the expert analyzes capital structure, liquidity, credit status, management depth, available cash flow, and other factors that may make the companies similar or dissimilar.

Lastly, the expert develops multiples from the guideline public companies. The multiples come from the relationship between their market price and some operating result such as sales or earnings. The guideline public company method uses multiples derived from the prices of comparable companies trading on the public markets. These valuation multiples are applied to the subject company to create an indication of value. Examples of types of multiples used are: price-to-revenues, price-to-net income, price-to-book value, etc. Although this method is used on large companies, using our examples, the results would be as follows:

Revenue	Net Income Scenario #1	Net Assets
$1,750,000	$117,000	$240,000
× 0.4	× 5	× 2
$700,000	$585,000	$480,000

We now move to the guideline transaction method.

Guideline transaction method. The guideline transaction method uses multiples derived from recent sales of comparable companies. These transactions are often of private companies purchased by public or private companies (but can be public-company acquisitions also). Use of this method has been facilitated, in recent years, by the development of databases that different information providers maintain and are available for purchase. These include *Pratt's Stats*, BIZCOMPS, Done Deals, Institute of Business Appraisers (IBA), Capital IQ, etc.

The problem with these databases is that they often have limited information, which makes the comparisons to the company being valued very difficult. Transaction databases rely upon private individuals and companies for information. They often provide selective disclosure of transaction details, which results in incomplete and inconsistent presentation of transaction data within each database. Furthermore, presentation of transaction details across databases varies. Some databases, such as *Pratt's Stats*, provide a large amount of detail, while others, such as IBA, provide only cursory information.

In addition, there is no way for the expert to know recent trends in the financial condition of each company reported and whether the transaction occurred at a high or low point in that company's operating cycle. Compounding the difficulty further, transaction negotiations often result in unique structures that may not be completely disclosed and/or do not lend themselves to comparison with other transactions—even within the same database. The following is a sample list of information that is usually not disclosed within certain databases but is relevant to determine comparability of the sale transaction:

1. Is the sale of assets or stock? (A stock sale would typically include all assets and liabilities of the company. In an asset sale, the owner often keeps certain assets, i.e., cash, and pays off the debt of the business).
2. For earnings multiples, what basis of earnings was utilized? (earnings before interest and taxes (EBIT), net income, owner's discretionary cash flow, etc.)
3. What assets are or are not included in the sales price?
4. What are the purchase terms of the sale (i.e., how much of a down payment was paid? Over how many years at what interest rate is the balance to be paid?)
5. Is there a noncompete agreement incorporated with the sale?
6. Will the selling owner continue to work at the company for an agreed amount of time and at a contracted amount of compensation?

As a consequence of these disparities, the guideline transaction method is rarely relied upon exclusively and is typically used as a check on the values the other methods indicate. Experts should be able to explain in detail why the subject company is comparable to the companies in the database. This method is best used in conjunction with another method, such as one of the methods under the income approach, and not as the sole method of valuation.

CASE STUDY: GUIDELINE TRANSACTION METHOD

Experts would value a retail store, such as the company in our case study, using the guideline transaction method as opposed to the guideline public company method. In our case study, Expert No. 1 uses a weighted average of the company's sales for the last five years, which equals $1,600,000. Expert No. 2 uses the current year's sales of $1,750,000. Expert No. 1 uses a multiple of 0.6 of revenues and does not include any assets. Expert No. 2 uses a multiple of 1.0 and adds in $150,000 for cash and receivables retained by the owner. The operation of this method is shown in the chart below.

TRANSACTION MULTIPLES COMPARISON

Measurement of Earnings	Expert No. 1	Expert No. 2	Judge
Sales	$1,600,000	$1,750,000	
Multiples	0.6	1.0	
Subtotal	960,000	1,750,000	
Treatment of excluded assets (liabilities)	-	150,000	
	$960,000	$1,900,000	

The difference between the experts is $940,000.

See Appendix 8 for a blank transaction multiples comparison chart that can be used to compare the experts' transaction multiples method.

The measurement of earnings does not have to be sales as used above. It can be another level of earnings. The experts will need to explain why they choose a certain level of earnings, how they picked their multiple, and why they believe certain assets were included or excluded from the sales price.

QUESTIONS TO ASK:

1. Is the sale of assets or stock?
2. For earnings multiples, what basis of earnings was utilized? (earnings before interests and taxes (EBIT), net income, owner's discretionary cash flow, etc.)
3. What assets are or are not included in the sales price?
4. What are the purchase terms of the sale (i.e., how much of a down payment was paid? Over how many years at what interest rate is the balance to be paid?)
5. Is there a noncompete agreement incorporated with the sale?
6. Will the selling owner continue to work at the company for an agreed amount of time and at a contracted amount of compensation?

SUMMARY

We prepared *The Business Valuation Bench Book* with two goals in mind. First, it should serve as a reference guide of fundamental business valuation concepts for judges who deal with the value of businesses and business interests in domestic and business disputes. Second, we sought to present a methodology whereby the trier of fact can separate a complex valuation into its component parts and analyze the expert's factual and theoretical support for his or her conclusions. As a reference guide, we explained the concepts used in the business valuation process, including: standards of value, premises of value, adjustments to income and expenses, and approaches and methods of value. We also identified the critical components of the valuation process including "normalized earnings," income to capitalize, the capitalization rate, and tax effects. We explained how even small changes in the critical components can have a significant effect on the conclusion of value. We also presented case studies of a clothing store and a real estate holding company to further illustrate these concepts.

To provide a methodology to identify the component parts in order to drill into the expert's factual and theoretical support for his or her conclusions, we included charts in the case studies that can be used to compare and contrast each expert's conclusions on the individual elements of his or her valuation. Using the explanations and questions presented in the relevant section of this book, the judge can use these charts, which are also presented as exhibits to this book, to assist in making findings of fact and conclusions of law.

We hope we have accomplished these goals and that you find this bench book helpful.

Appendix 1. Charting Goodwill Jurisprudence (as of March 2017)

Appraisers working on divorce cases know that goodwill is a fundamental concept they have to master. What makes it challenging is that divorce is a state matter and that different states adhere to different rules as to how to treat goodwill.

Business Valuation Resources has updated its handy reference guide (formerly known as "Goodwill Hunting in Divorce")—a state-by-state breakdown of goodwill jurisprudence. Practitioners learn at a glance what a state's basic position toward enterprise and professional goodwill is and can shape their valuations accordingly.

We have expanded our discussion of the law to include excerpts from foundational cases that highlight the concepts (e.g., salability, transferability, solo practice, noncompete agreements) underlying a state's position. The additional information gives insight into how different courts emphasize different concepts and how much discussion there is within a jurisdiction around the basic rule.

Ideally, this chart becomes a real-time guide. We, therefore, welcome alerts to precedent-making new cases or legislative changes.

Here we say special thanks to the following experts for assisting with the research: Jim Alerding (Alerding Consulting, LLC), Christine Baker (Charter Capital Partners), Tom Burrage (The Forensic Firm), Cindy Craig (Cynthia V. Craig, CPA), Don Drysdale (Drysdale Valuation), Jay Fishman (Financial Research Associates), Gary Freeman (Regier Carr & Monroe, LLP), Lynne Gold-Bikin (Weber Gallagher), Ted Israel (Israel Frey Group, LLP), Rob Levis (Levis Consulting), Harold Martin (Keiter), Tom Napier (Napier & Company, LLC), Forrest W. (Bo), Olson (Olson Neaves & Company, P.C.), Ron Seigneur (Seigneur Gustafson LLP), Jeff Tarbell (Houlihan Lokey), Gary Trugman (Trugman Valuation Associates, Inc.), Stacey Udell (Gold Gerstein Group LLC).

Sylvia Golden, Esq.,
EXECUTIVE LEGAL EDITOR

STATE	POSITION	CASES	TYPE OF PRACTICE	BV LAW*
ALABAMA	No decision			
ALASKA	Enterprise goodwill is marital, personal goodwill is not. Distinguishing marketable from unmarketable goodwill; only marketable goodwill is part of marital estate.	*Moffit v. Moffit,* 749 P.2d 343 (Alaska 1988)	Contracting business	Yes
	It may be that marketable professional goodwill exists in a multilawyer firm, for example, upon evidence of sales or purchases of partnership interests.	*Richmond v. Richmond,* 779 P.2d 1211 (Alaska)	Law firm	Yes
ARIZONA	Personal and enterprise goodwill are marital; goodwill in professional partnership is community asset.	*Mitchell v. Mitchell,* 732 P.2d 208 (Ariz. 1987)	Accounting practice	Yes
	Discussing solo practice and rejecting trial court's ruling that a professional corporation "is directly and literally tied to the life of [the] owner spouse"; setting forth factors to determine goodwill of professional corporation.	*Compare Wisner v. Wisner,* 129 Ariz. 333 (App. 1981)	Medical practice	Yes
	Goodwill analysis not limited to "realizable benefits."	*Walsh v. Walsh,* 2012 Ariz. App. LEXIS 162	Law office	Yes
ARKANSAS	Enterprise goodwill is marital; personal goodwill is not.	*Wilson v. Wilson,* 294 Ark. 194 (1987)	Orthopedic surgery	Yes
	Discussing whether personal goodwill can be found in non-professional practices, such as a restaurant.	*Brave v. Brave,* 2014 Ark. 175	Restaurant	Yes

* BVLaw is available with a subscription at BVLibrary.com/bvlaw.

STATE	POSITION	CASES	TYPE OF PRACTICE	BV LAW*
CALIFORNIA	If community property, no distinction between enterprise and personal goodwill. If separate property interest involved, more nuanced analysis.			
	Goodwill can also exist in a professional practice that is founded on personal skill or reputation.	*Mueller v. Mueller,* 144 Cal. App. 2d 245 (1956)	Dental lab	Yes
	Goodwill of husband's professional practice as a sole practitioner should be considered in determining award to wife.	*Golden v. Golden,* 270 Cal. App. 2d 401 (1969)	Medical practice	Yes
	Consistent with concept of community property, if professional goodwill is found to exist as an asset at the time of marital dissolution, it may be separate property, community property, or varying degrees of both depending on particular circumstances. No rigid rule for determining the existence or value of the "goodwill" of a law practice or any other profession as a going-concern business. States factors contributing to value of professional goodwill.	*In re Lopez,* 38 Cal. 3d 93 (1974)	Law practice	No

* BVLaw is available with a subscription at BVLibrary.com/bvlaw.

STATE	POSITION	CASES	TYPE OF PRACTICE	BV LAW*
COLORADO	No distinction; personal and enterprise goodwill are marital. Value of goodwill incident to husband's practice, which is an asset acquired during marriage, must be considered marital property.	*In re Marriage of Nichols,* 43 Colo. App. 383 (1979)	Dental practice	Yes
	Goodwill of an ongoing business that is acquired during marriage is an intangible asset to be considered in division of marital property.	*In re Marriage of Martin,* 707 P.2d 1035 (1985)	Accounting firm	No
	An individual practitioner's inability to sell a law practice does not eliminate existence of goodwill and its value as an asset to be considered in equitable distribution.	*In re Marriage of Huff,* 834 P.2d 244 (1992)	Law firm	Yes
CONNECTICUT	Enterprise goodwill is marital; personal goodwill is not. Value of goodwill must be determined on the basis of the price a willing buyer would pay in excess of tangible assets.	*Eslami v. Eslami,* 591 A.2d. 411 (Conn. 1991)	Medical practice	Yes
DELAWARE	Enterprise goodwill is marital; personal goodwill is not.	*E.E.C. v. E.J.C.,* 457 A.2d 688 (Del. 1983)	Law practice	No
DISTRICT OF COLUMBIA	Enterprise goodwill is marital; personal goodwill is not. Goodwill of a professional practice acquired during marriage is an asset subject to distribution. Depending on facts of the case, a professional practice may have no goodwill value.	*McDiarmid v. McDiarmid,* 649 A. 2d 810 (D.C. App. 1994)	Law practice	Yes

* BVLaw is available with a subscription at BVLibrary.com/bvlaw.

STATE	POSITION	CASES	TYPE OF PRACTICE	BV LAW*
FLORIDA	Enterprise goodwill is marital; personal goodwill is not.	*Thompson v. Thompson,* 576 So. 2d 267 (Fla. 1991)	Law practice	Yes
	For purpose of distinguishing enterprise from personal goodwill, there is no distinction between nonsolicitation/ nonpiracy agreements and covenant not to compete; all are indicative of personal goodwill.	*Held v. Held*, 2005 Fla. App. LEXIS 14138	Insurance agency	Yes
GEORGIA	Enterprise goodwill is marital; personal goodwill is not.	*Miller v. Miller,* 2010 WL 4704326 (Ga.) (Nov. 22, 2010)	Medical practice	Yes
HAWAII	Enterprise goodwill is marital; personal goodwill is not. "True goodwill" of a business is a marketable business asset. Goodwill that depends on continued presence of owner spouse is not marketable asset distinct from owner.	*Antolik v. Harvey,* 761 P. 2d 305 (Haw. App. 1988)	Chiropractic business	Yes
IDAHO	Majority declines to distinguish personal and business goodwill and rejects distinction between professional practices and other businesses; dissent strongly disagrees.	*Stewart v. Stewart,* 2007 Ida. LEXIS 17 (Jan. 26, 2007)	Dermatology practice	Yes
ILLINOIS	Enterprise goodwill is marital; personal is not.	*In re Marriage of Head,* 652 N.E. 2d 1246 (Ill. App. 1995)	Medical practice	Yes
INDIANA	Enterprise goodwill is marital, but "even a professional can have an enterprise goodwill component to its value"; where goodwill is attributable to owner as an individual, it is not marital.	*Yoon v. Yoon,* 711 N.E.2d 1265 (1999)	Medical practice	Yes
	A party wanting to exclude personal goodwill from a business valuation must submit evidence of its existence and its value to the trial court.	*Balicki v. Balicki,* 837 N.E.2d 532, (Ind. App. 2005)	Mechanical/ construction	Yes

* BVLaw is available with a subscription at BVLibrary.com/bvlaw.

STATE	POSITION	CASES	TYPE OF PRACTICE	BV LAW*
IOWA	Treatment of goodwill is unclear. Goodwill in a professional practice depends on professional's continuing in practice; if practice owned with other professionals, goodwill also is dependent on relationship with other professionals; to the extent it exists, it is a factor bearing on professional's future earning potential.	*In re Marriage of Hogeland,* 448 N.W.2d 678 (Iowa App. 1989)	Dental practice	No
	Iowa courts are not prohibited from considering goodwill or future earning capacity when valuing a law practice.	*In re Marriage of Barten,* 2010 Iowa App. LEXIS 670	Law practice	Yes
KANSAS	Professional goodwill that is marketable is marital property. "All property owned by married persons ... including for divorce or separate maintenance actions commenced on or after July 1, 1998, professional goodwill to the extent it is marketable for that particular professional ... shall become marital property."	Kan. Stat. Ann. Section 23-2801(a)		
KENTUCKY	Enterprise goodwill is marital; personal goodwill is not.	*Gaskill v. Robbins,* 2009 WL 425619 (Ky.) (Feb. 19, 2009)	Medical practice	Yes
	Distinguishing between professional practice and nonprofessional practice; in nonprofessional practice, goodwill likely is enterprise goodwill.	*Rabe v. Rabe,* 2015 Ky. App. Unpub. LEXIS 379	Transportation business	Yes

* BVLaw is available with a subscription at BVLibrary.com/bvlaw.

STATE	POSITION	CASES	TYPE OF PRACTICE	BV LAW*
LOUISIANA	Enterprise goodwill is marital; personal goodwill is not.	Statute: La. R.S. 9:2801.2 added by Acts 2003, No. 837 § 1 and amended by Acts 2004, No. 177 § 1		
	Where one spouse holds a professional degree or license and the goodwill results solely from that spouse's personal relationship with clients, it is not community property.	*Stratham v. Stratham,* 2008 La. App. LEXIS 939	Insurance broker	No
MAINE	Enterprise goodwill is marital; personal goodwill is not.	*Ahern v. Ahern,* 2008 Me. LEXIS 1 (Jan. 3, 2008)	Dental practice	Yes
MARYLAND	Enterprise goodwill is marital; personal goodwill is not. There may be a degree of likelihood that goodwill exists as a valuable asset of a law firm, but "it is doubtful that the practice of a sole practitioner enjoys any marketable goodwill."	*Prahinski v. Prahinski,* 75 Md. App. 113 (1987))	Law practice	No
	We are not convinced that the goodwill of a solo law practice can be separated from the reputation of the attorney. Accordingly, goodwill is attributable to attorney and not divisible.	*Prahinski v. Prahinski,* 321 Md. 227 (1990)	Law practice	No
MASSACHUSETTS	Enterprise goodwill is marital; personal goodwill is not.	*Goldman v. Goldman,* 554 N.E.2d 860 (Mass. App. 1990)	Medical practice	No
MICHIGAN	No distinction; personal and enterprise goodwill are marital.	*Kowalesky v. Kowalesky,* 384 N.W.2d 112 (Mich. App. 1986)	Dental practice	No
MINNESOTA	Enterprise goodwill is marital; personal goodwill is not.	*Roth v. Roth,* 406 N.W.2d 77 (Minn. App. 1987)	Chiropractic business	No

* BVLaw is available with a subscription at BVLibrary.com/bvlaw.

STATE	POSITION	CASES	TYPE OF PRACTICE	BV LAW*
MISSISSIPPI	Neither personal nor enterprise goodwill is marital. Goodwill should not be used in determining the fair market value of a business, subject to equitable division in divorce cases.	*Singley v. Singley,* 848 So. 2d 1004 (Miss. 2002)	Dental practice	Yes
	Although there is a distinction between "personal goodwill" and "business enterprise goodwill," neither should be included in valuing a solo practice.	*Watson v. Watson,* 882 So.2d 95 (Miss. 2004)	Veterinary clinic	Yes
MISSOURI	Enterprise goodwill is marital; personal goodwill is not. Goodwill in a professional practice is a marital asset subject to division; fair market value evidence indicates no goodwill value in the partnership.	*Hanson v. Hanson,* 738 S.W.2d 429 (Mo. 1987)	Medical practice (oral surgical partnership)	Yes
MONTANA	No distinction; personal and enterprise goodwill are marital. Goodwill of a professional anesthesiology practice may be a martial asset subject to property division.	*In re Marriage of Hull,* 219 Mont. 480 (1986)	Medical practice	Yes
NEBRASKA	Enterprise goodwill is marital; personal goodwill is not. To be a divisible asset, "goodwill must be a business asset with value independent of the presence or reputation of a particular individual, an asset which may be sold ... or pledged."	*Taylor v. Taylor,* 386 N.W. 2d 851 (Neb. 1986)	Medical practice	Yes

* BVLaw is available with a subscription at BVLibrary.com/bvlaw.

STATE	POSITION	CASES	TYPE OF PRACTICE	BV LAW*
NEVADA	No distinction; personal and enterprise goodwill are marital. We adopt the modern rule that would include a professional practice's goodwill as part of the community property estate subject to division.	*Ford v. Ford,* 782 P.2d 1304 (Nev. 1989)	Medical practice	Yes
NEW HAMPSHIRE	Enterprise goodwill is marital; personal goodwill is not. Trial court could reasonably have determined it was inappropriate to place a value on goodwill of the practice where the partnership agreement does not require owner-spouse to execute a covenant not to compete upon sale of stock.	*In re Watterworth,* 821 A. 2d 1107 (N.H. 2003)	Medical practice	Yes
NEW JERSEY	No distinction; personal and enterprise goodwill are marital. Goodwill may be present whether that form is a partnership, corporation, joint venture, or individual proprietorship. Moreover, goodwill exists in personal service enterprises as well as other businesses.	*Dugan v. Dugan,* 457 A.2d 1 (N.J. 1983)	Law practice	Yes
NEW MEXICO	No distinction; personal and enterprise goodwill are marital. Goodwill is community property divisible upon divorce.	*Mitchell v. Mitchell,* 719 P.2d 432 (N.M. App. 1986)	Accounting practice	Yes
	Salability is not decisive factor; doctor's goodwill has value despite its immarketability.	*Hurley v. Hurley,* 615 P.2d 256 (N.M. 1980)	Medical practice	Yes

* BVLaw is available with a subscription at BVLibrary.com/bvlaw.

STATE	POSITION	CASES	TYPE OF PRACTICE	BV LAW*
NEW YORK	No distinction; personal and enterprise goodwill are marital. "'Marital property' is defined to mean 'all property acquired by either or both spouses during marriage and before *** the commencement of a matrimonial action.'"	*Nehorayeff v. Nehorayeff,* 108 Misc. 2d 311 (1981) (citing Domestic Relations Law, § 236)	Medical practice	No
	A medical license is marital property. "There is no reason in law or logic to restrict the plain language of the statute to existing practices.... An established practice merely represents the exercise of the privileges conferred upon the professional spouse by the license."	*O'Brien v. O'Brien,* 66.N.Y.2d 576 (1985)	Medical license	No
	Stockbroker's "book of business" equates to professional goodwill and is marital property as contemplated by the applicable domestic relations law.	*Moll v. Moll,* 722 N.Y.S. 2d 732 (2001)	Stockbroker	Yes
NORTH CAROLINA	No distinction; personal and enterprise goodwill are marital. "[G]oodwill is an asset that must be valued and considered in determining the value of a professional practice for purposes of equitable [421] distribution."	*Poore v. Poore,* 331 S.E.2d 266 (N.C. App. 1985)	Dental practice	Yes
NORTH DAKOTA	No distinction; personal and enterprise goodwill are marital. The fact that a party's earning power or entrepreneurial skill is not property should not "be taken as an indication that the goodwill of [a party's] business interests should not be considered in determining the value of the parties' property."	*Nastrom v. Nastrom,* 262 N.W. 487 (N.D. 1978)	Medical practice	Yes

* BVLaw is available with a subscription at BVLibrary.com/bvlaw.

STATE	POSITION	CASES	TYPE OF PRACTICE	BV LAW*
OHIO	Personal and enterprise goodwill in professional practice is marital. Goodwill is an integral part of the valuation of a professional business in a divorce proceeding.	*Kahn v. Kahn*, 42 Ohio App. 3d 61 (1987)	Medical practice	Yes
	Court says there are problems with valuing the goodwill of a solo practice "because any goodwill would be personal to the individual doctor such that it would be unalienable and untransferable."	*Goswami v. Goswami*, 152 Ohio App. 3d 151 (2003)	Medical practice	Yes
	Court limits personal goodwill to value of covenant not to compete in actual sale of owner-spouse's practice. A covenant not to compete represents a nonmarital asset.	*Banchefsky v. Banchefsky*, 2010-Ohio-4267	Dental practice	Yes
OKLAHOMA	Enterprise goodwill is marital; personal is not. Goodwill of medical practice is marital property as it is distinct from owner spouse's personal reputation; indeed owner may use goodwill as selling point to potential buyers.	*Traczyk v. Traczyk*, 891 P.2d 1277 (Okla. 1995)	Medical practice (podiatry clinic)	Yes
	No marital goodwill where the business is a medical practice owned by a group of stockholder physicians and husband could recoup goodwill value only by continuing to work with the business.	*Compare Mocnik v. Mocnik*, 838 P.2 500 (Okla. 1992)	Medical practice	Yes
	Solo law practice has no goodwill value for purposes of marital property because goodwill is not distinct from lawyer's reputation.	*Travis v. Travis*, 795 P.2d 96 (Okla. 1990)	Law practice	Yes

* BVLaw is available with a subscription at BVLibrary.com/bvlaw.

STATE	POSITION	CASES	TYPE OF PRACTICE	BV LAW*
OREGON	Enterprise goodwill is marital; personal is not. When valuing business as a marital asset, it is improper to assume owner will execute a covenant not to compete; value of CNTC indicative of personal goodwill.	*Slater v. Slater*, 245 P.3d 676 (2010)	Chiropractic clinic	Yes
PENNSYLVANIA	Enterprise goodwill is marital; personal goodwill is not. Decision of whether a business has goodwill is controlled by the nature of the business itself.	*Solomon v. Solomon*, 611 A.2d 686 (1990)	Equine clinic	No
	If economic goodwill is purely personal to the professional spouse, it is not alienable and not includable in equitable distribution; if a portion is attributable to the business and can be realized by sale to another, goodwill is subject to equitable distribution.	*Fexa v. Fexa*, 578 A.2d 1314 (1990)	Dental practice	Yes
	Goodwill of a personal nature should not be considered for purposes of equitable distribution.	*Butler v Butler*, 663 A.2d 148 (Pa. 1995)	Accounting firm	Yes
RHODE ISLAND	Enterprise goodwill is marital; personal goodwill is not. In evaluating goodwill as a company asset, it is important to distinguish between personal and enterprise goodwill.	*Moretti v. Moretti*, 766 A.2d 925 (R.I. 2001)	Professional landscaper	Yes
SOUTH CAROLINA	Enterprise goodwill is marital; personal goodwill is not. "Accordingly, we elect to follow the emerging majority approach and hold enterprise goodwill is marital property subject to equitable division." "We continue to hold that personal goodwill ... is not marital property subject to division."	*Moore v. Moore*, 2015 S.C. LEXIS 343	Retail store (lighting fixtures, home furnishings)	Yes

* BVLaw is available with a subscription at BVLibrary.com/bvlaw.

STATE	POSITION	CASES	TYPE OF PRACTICE	BV LAW*
SOUTH DAKOTA	Enterprise goodwill in professional practice is marital. In the instant case, including goodwill in the valuation of the business was not error where there was sufficient evidence of its value, including its reputation in the community. But court expressly declined to decide whether personal goodwill in professional practice is marital property.	*Endres v. Endres*, 532 N.W.2d (S.D. 1995)	Dairy and concrete business	Yes
TENNESSEE	Typically, enterprise goodwill is not marital asset where the business involved is a sole proprietorship. But some shift, depending on facts of the case.	*Smith v. Smith*, 709 S.W.2d 588 (1985)	Law practice	Yes
	Thus, the professional goodwill is not a marital asset, which would be accounted for in making an equitable distribution of the marital estate.	*Hartline v. Hartline*, 2014 Tenn. App. LEXIS 7	Dental practice	Yes
	Where husband is sole practitioner of an unincorporated dental practice, goodwill, whether personal or associated with practice, is not a marital asset.	*Lunn v. Lunn*, 2015 Tenn. App. LEXIS 515	Dental practice	Yes
	Where business is an incorporated multispecialty medical group, valuation not limited to net asset value.	*Compare York v. York*, 1992 Tenn. App. LEXIS 661	Medical clinic	Yes
	Goodwill in solo financial planning practice is not marital asset but trail income generated from ongoing management of client funds and accounts is marital property. Controlling factor is that trail income could be sold separately, court says.	*Compare Fuller v. Fuller*, 2016 Tenn. App. LEXIS 974	Financial planning practice	Yes

* BVLaw is available with a subscription at BVLibrary.com/bvlaw.

STATE	POSITION	CASES	TYPE OF PRACTICE	BV LAW*
TEXAS	Enterprise goodwill is marital; personal goodwill is not. Goodwill in a solo practice is not divisible. Case not concerned with goodwill in a professional partnership or corporation apart from the person of an individual member.	*Nail v. Nail,* 486 S.W.2d 761 (Tex. 1972)	Medical practice	Yes
	Corporation has goodwill separate and apart from the goodwill attributable to the owner-spouse.	*Geesbreght v. Geesbreght,* 570 S.W.2d 427 (1978)	Physicians practice (emergency room services)	No
	Extent of husband's interest in law firm's goodwill is governed by partnership agreement.	*Finn v. Finn,* 658 S.W.2d 735 (1983)	Law firm	No
UTAH	Enterprise goodwill is marital; personal goodwill is not. Finding goodwill and reputation of a sole practitioner are not marital property.	*Sorensen v. Sorensen,* 839 P.2d 774 (Utah 1992)	Dental practice	Yes
	Appeals court lets stand trial court's ruling that business's value was "solely attributable to [Husband's] personal, professional reputation."	*Stonehocker v. Stonehocker,* 2008 Utah App. LEXIS 10	Car dealership	No
VERMONT	Enterprise goodwill is marital, personal goodwill is not. Where attorney works as contract attorney, her services have no independent value beyond her ability to perform them.	*Mills v. Mills,* 167 Vt. 567 (1997)	Contract lawyer	No
VIRGINIA	Enterprise goodwill is marital; personal goodwill is not.	*Howell v. Howell,* 31 Va. App. 332 (2000)	Law practice	Yes
	Finding owner spouse failed to show that prevailing valuation included owner's personal goodwill	*See also Hoebelheinrich v. Hoebelheinrich,* 43 Va App. 543 (2004)	Medical practice	Yes

* BVLaw is available with a subscription at BVLibrary.com/bvlaw.

STATE	POSITION	CASES	TYPE OF PRACTICE	BV LAW*
WASHINGTON	No distinction; personal and enterprise goodwill are marital. Finding professional goodwill is to be included in property division; goodwill may exist even if it's not readily marketable.	*In re Marriage of Lukens*, 16 Wn. App. 481 (1976)	Medical practice	No
	The value of goodwill to the professional spouse ... constitutes a community asset and should be considered by the court in distributing the community property.	*See also In re Marriage of Fleege,* 91 Wn.2d 324 (1979)	Dental practice	Yes
WEST VIRGINIA	Enterprise goodwill is marital; personal goodwill is not. In determining whether goodwill should be valued for purposes of equitable distribution, courts must look to the precise nature of that goodwill.	*May v. May,* 214 W. Va 394 (2003)	Dental practice	Yes
WISCONSIN	Distinguishing salable from nonsalable goodwill and finding salable professional goodwill is divisible and includable in the marital estate.	*McReath v. McReath,* 2011 Wisc. LEXIS 354 (July 12, 2011)	Dental practice	Yes
	Addressing nonsalable professional goodwill only.	*Compare Holbrook v. Holbrook,* 103 Wis. 2d 327 (Ct. App. 1981)	Law practice	No
WYOMING	Enterprise goodwill is marital; personal goodwill is not. No goodwill value to business where its income depends solely on work and skills of owner-spouse. "These are not assets that can be sold to another physician."	*Root v. Root,* 65 P.3d 41 (Wyo. 2003)	Medical practice	Yes

* BVLaw is available with a subscription at BVLibrary.com/bvlaw.

Appendix 2. Normalization Adjustments Comparison

	Expert No. 1	Expert No. 2	Judge
Net Income			
Adjustments			
Add or (subtract)			
Add: reported compensation			
Less: reasonable compensation			
Income before tax			

Appendix 3. Income to Capitalize Comparison

Year	Expert No. 1	Expert No. 2	Judge
1			
2			
3			
4			
5			
Divided by			
Pretax income to capitalize			
Taxes			
After-tax income to capitalize			
Other (i.e., projection)			

Appendix 4. Cap Rate Comparison

	Expert No. 1	Expert No. 2	Judge
Risk-free rate			
+ Equity risk			
± Industry risk			
+ Size premium			
Specific company risk			
Discount rate			
Less: growth rate			
Cap rate			

Appendix 5. Discounted Cash Flow Comparison

	Year	Expert No. 1		Expert No. 2		Judge	
		Amount	%	Amount	%	Amount	%
Normalized pretax income							
Sales growth							
(% growth)							
	1						
	2						
	3						
	4						
Cost of sales							
(% growth)							
	1						
	2						
	3						
	4						
Operating expenses							
(% growth)							
	1						
	2						
	3						
	4						
Tax rate							
Discount rate							
Terminal value							
Discount rate							
Less: long-term growth							
Cap rate							

Appendix 6. Net Assets Comparison

	Expert No. 1	Expert No. 2	Judge
Assets			
Cash			
Rent receivable			
Note			
Building			
Liabilities			
Accounts payable			
Mortgage			
Net equity			

Appendix 7. Excess Earnings Comparison

		Expert No. 1		Expert No. 2		Judge
Income to capitalize						
Less rate of return on net tangible assets	%		%		%	
Excess earnings						
Divided by: capitalization rate						
Goodwill value						
Plus: net tangible assets						
Company value						

Appendix 8. Transaction Multiples Comparison

Measurement of Earnings	Expert No. 1	Expert No. 2	Judge
Sales			
Multiples			
Subtotal			
Treatment of excluded assets (liabilities)			

Appendix 9. The Basics of Discounts

Two primary types of discounts are applied to the value of a fractional interest in a privately held company. These discounts are the discount for lack of control and the discount for lack of marketability.

All discounts should also be examined in the context of the standard of value being applied and jurisdictional rules and precedents. In many, but not all, jurisdictions with a fair market value standard of value, the application of discounts for both lack of control and lack of marketability may be considered. In many, but not all, jurisdictions, when using a fair value standard in connection with dissent and oppression cases, no discounts are considered. However, in some states, one or both may still be applied. In several other states, such as New Jersey, minority discounts are not applied and marketability discounts are only applied if there are extraordinary circumstances.

Levels of Value[1]

The chart below illustrates "levels of value," or the value result using certain methods and approaches to valuation. The chart illustrates the levels at which certain premiums or discounts are applicable. It is important that premiums and discounts, if applied, are applied only against the appropriate level of value. For example purposes only, the per-share prices are:

Synergistic value	$12.00	
		Strategic acquisition premium
Control shares value	$10.00	
		Control premium ↑ Discount for lack of control ↓
Publicly traded equivalent value	$8.00	
		Discount for lack of marketability for restricted stock
Restricted stock of public companies value	$6.00	
		Additional discount for lack of marketability for private-company stock
Nonmarketable minority value	$4.40	

1 Jay E. Fishman, Shannon P. Pratt, J. Clifford Griffith, and James R. Hitchner, *PPC's Guide to Business Valuations*, 26th edition, Thomson Reuters, February 2016, pages 8-14.

Discount for Lack of Control

The *International Glossary of Business Valuation Terms* defines the discount for lack of control (DLOC) as:

> An amount or percentage deducted from the pro rata share of value of 100 percent of an equity interest in a business to reflect the absence of some or all of the powers of control.[2]

There are many possible powers of control and degrees of those powers. For example, the ability to appoint or change management or determine management compensation and perquisites may be evidence of some control, and the lack thereof is evidence of no control. However, the holder of the interest being valued may have a level of partial control over management and its compensation through its minority shareholding such as sharing the decision-making process or having to vote with other shareholders. This interest would have a lower DLOC than one without any powers of control. The expert must consider whether the interest being valued has all, some, or no powers of control. The expert should clearly explain the powers of control, or lack thereof, which he or she identified in reaching his or her conclusion of a DLOC.

The following are examples of some powers of control and degrees of control.

Powers of control examples:[3]

- Appoint or change operational management;
- Appoint or change members of the board of directors;
- Determine management compensation and perquisites;
- Set operational and strategic policy and change the course of the business;
- Acquire, lease, or liquidate business assets, including plant, property, and equipment;
- Select suppliers, vendors, and subcontractors with whom to do business and award contracts;

2 American Society of Appraisers, Business Valuation Standards, 2009, from the *International Glossary of Business Valuation Terms*.

3 Shannon P. Pratt with Alina V. Niculita, *Valuing a Business: The Analysis and Appraisal of Closely Held Companies*, 5th edition, The McGraw-Hill Companies Inc., 2008, Chapter 15, "Control and Acquisition Premiums," page 385.

- Negotiate and consummate mergers and acquisitions;
- Liquidate, dissolve, sell out, or recapitalize the company;
- Sell or acquire Treasury shares;
- Register the company's equity securities for an initial or secondary public offering;
- Register the company's debt securities for an initial or secondary public offering;
- Declare and pay cash and/or stock dividends;
- Change the articles of incorporation or bylaws;
- Set one's own compensation (and perquisites) and the compensation (and perquisites) of related-party employees;
- Select joint ventures and enter into joint venture and partnership agreements;
- Decide what products and/or services to offer and how to price those products/services;
- Decide what markets and locations to serve, to enter into, and to discontinue serving;
- Decide which customer categories to market to and which not to market to;
- Enter into inbound and outbound license or sharing agreements regarding intellectual properties; and
- Block any of the above actions.

Degree of control examples:[4]

- Cumulative voting versus noncumulative voting;
- Contractual restrictions;
- Effects of regulations, including state statutes;

4 Jay E. Fishman, Shannon P. Pratt, J. Clifford Griffith, James R. Hitchner, *PPC's Guide to Business Valuations,* 26th edition, Thomson Reuters, February 2016, pages 8-15 to 8-16.

- Financial condition of the business; and
- Effects of distribution of ownership.

Control Premiums

Control premiums are seen in the marketplace when controlling interests in public companies are acquired; that is, the price the acquirer paid exceeds the price at which the individual shares are trading in the market. The excess above the stock price is the acquisition premium and contains anticipated synergistic benefits from the acquisition and also may include a control premium. DLOCs are the inverse of control premiums and are derived from marketplace acquisition premiums without the ability to specifically identify the control premium component.

Sources of DLOCs

The following are the primary sources of DLOCs:

- *Mergerstat® Review* is published annually by Business Valuation Resources and FactSet Mergerstat LLC. *Mergerstat® Review* provides information concerning the premiums for control and implied minority interest discounts from market transactions; and
- Mergerstat®/BVR Control Premium Study™. This is an online source providing a database of premiums and discounts from market transactions.

Application of DLOCs

As mentioned previously, minority owners may have some or none of the powers of control. The prerogatives of control minority shareholders hold should be assessed when selecting a DLOC and only be applied to a control share's value.

However, another method for assessing the cash flows to a minority shareholder is through adjusting the expected cash flows to minority cash flows rather than applying a calculated DLOC percentage.

Either way, the resultant value after the application of a DLOC or the cash flows adjustment should represent the cash that flows through to the respective minority shareholder.

Discount for Lack of Marketability

The *International Glossary of Business Valuation Terms* defines the discount for lack of marketability (DLOM) as:

> An amount or percentage deducted from the value of an ownership interest to reflect the relative absence of marketability.[5]

The American Society of Appraisers defines marketability as:

> The capability and ease of transfer or salability of an asset, business, business ownership interest, security or intangible asset" and has "the ability to quickly convert property to cash at minimal cost."[6]

As reflected in the "Levels of Value" chart above, ownership interests in restricted stock of public companies or shares in privately held companies have a lower value than the publicly traded value due to the inability to sell these interests quickly or easily. For instance, restricted stock may have required holding periods or privately held shares may reacquire substantial due diligence by a potential buyer before a sale can occur.

Factors Affecting Size of DLOM

Some of the factors that affect the size of the discount for lack of marketability were delineated in the *Mandelbaum et al. v. Commissioner* case:[7]

- Financial statement analysis;
- Dividend policy;
- Nature of the company, its history, its position in the industry, and its economic outlook;

5 Ibid.
6 American Society of Appraisers, Business Valuation Standards, Glossary, November 2009.
7 *Mandelbaum et al. v. Commissioner*, T.C. Memo 1995-255. Appealed and affirmed, 91 F.3d 124, 1996 U.S. App. LEXUS 17962, 96-2 U.S. Tax Cas. (CCH) P60, 240, 78 A.F.T.R. 2d (RIA) 5159.

- Management;
- Amount of control in the transferred shares;
- Restrictions on transferability;
- Holding period for the stock;
- Company's redemption policy; and
- Costs associated with a public offering.

An expanded list of factors was delineated in the *Discount for Lack of Marketability Job Aid for IRS Valuation Professionals:*[8]

Subject company factors:

- Value of subject corporation's privately traded securities versus its publicly traded securities;
- Dividend-paying (or distribution) ability and history;
- Dividend yield;
- Attractiveness of subject business;
- Attractiveness of subject industry;
- Prospects for a sale or public offering of the company;
- Number of identifiable buyers;
- Attributes of controlling shareholder, if any;
- Availability of access to information or reliability of that information;
- Management;
- Earnings levels;
- Revenue levels;
- Book-to-market value ratios;

8 *Discount for Lack of Marketability Job Aid for IRS Valuation Professional,* Sept. 25, 2009.

- Information requirements;
- Ownership concentration effects;
- Financial condition;
- Percentage of shares held by insiders;
- Percentage of shares held by institutions;
- Percentage of independent directors;
- Listing on a major exchange;
- Active versus passive investors;
- Registration costs;
- Availability of hedging opportunities;
- Market capitalization rank; and
- Business risk.

Subject interest factors:

- Restrictive transfer provisions;
- Length of the restriction period;
- Length of the expected holding period;
- Offering size as a percentage of total shares outstanding; and
- Registered versus unregistered.

While the above are not all inclusive and many of the delineated factors may even be duplicative, an expert should assess and discuss these factors when selecting a DLOM.

A DLOM is applied by first determining the levels of value starting point such as control value then evaluating the marketability of the respective interest. DLOMs are applied after DLOCs, if applicable.[9]

9 DLOCs and DLOMs are not additive. A DLOC is first applied, and a DLOM is applied to that resulting value.

Sources of DLOMs

The traditional view of selecting DLOMs is examining shares in the marketplace that have trading restrictions and comparing those prices to the corresponding publicly traded prices and assuming that the difference represents the DLOM. The areas that are focused on here are restricted stock studies and preinitial public offering (pre-IPO) studies. In recent years, the ability to search databases for specific restricted stock and pre-IPO transactions has provided additional support for selected DLOMs.

A more recent view of selecting DLOMs is through financial derivatives. Certain hedging instruments were established to limit risk and/or protect one from loss in value. In recent years, a number of hedging strategies using option pricing models have been proposed as providing a basis for a DLOM. These include the Chaffee model, the Longstaff option pricing model, and put options and collars such as long-term equity anticipation securities (LEAPs), and variable prepaid forward contracts.

Finally, there are numerous other studies and other approaches to selecting DLOMs such as QMDM, NICE, NERA, and Partnership Profiles.

Other Discounts

There are several other possible types of discounts including, but not limited to, the following:

- Discount for lack of liquidity;
- Discount for lack of voting rights;
- Blockage discount;
- Key person, or customer, or product discount;
- Built-in capital gains discount; and
- Environmental liability discount.

These discounts relate to events that may affect the value at which a willing buyer and willing seller would transact an interest. These discounts are not unusual, but they depend on specific circumstances. Their use and size should be supported in detail by the expert that utilizes them.

Appendix 10. Glossary of Business Valuation Terms

To enhance and sustain the quality of business valuations for the benefit of the profession and its clientele, the American Institute of Certified Public Accountants, American Society of Appraisers, Canadian Institute of Chartered Business Valuators, and the National Association of Certified Valuation Analysts have adopted the definitions for the terms included in this glossary, unless otherwise credited to another source. If another source was used other than the original *International Glossary of Business Valuation Terms*, the source will be noted in parentheses after the term is defined.

The performance of business valuation services requires a high degree of skill and imposes upon the valuation professional a duty to communicate the valuation process and conclusion in a manner that is clear and not misleading. This duty is advanced through the use of terms whose meanings are clearly established and consistently applied throughout the profession.

If, in the opinion of the business valuation professional, one or more of these terms needs to be used in a manner that materially departs from the enclosed definitions, it is recommended that the term be defined as used within that valuation engagement.

This glossary has been developed to provide guidance to business valuation practitioners by further memorializing the body of knowledge that constitutes the competent and careful determination of value and, more particularly, the communication of how that value was determined.

Departure from this glossary is not intended to provide a basis for civil liability and should not be presumed to create evidence that any duty has been breached.

Accounts payable—an accounting entry that represents an entity's obligation to pay off a short-term debt to its creditors. The accounts payable entry is found on a balance sheet under the heading "current liabilities." (*investopedia.com*)

Accounts receivable—money owed by customers (individuals or corporations) to another entity in exchange for goods or services that have been delivered or used but not yet paid for. Receivables usually come in the form of operating lines of credit and are usually due within a relatively short time period, ranging from a few days to a year. (*investopedia.com*)

Adjusted book value method—a method within the asset approach whereby all assets and liabilities (including off-balance sheet, intangible, and contingent) are adjusted to their fair market values (*Note: In Canada, on a going-concern basis*).

Adjusted net asset method—see **Adjusted book value method.**

AM (*Accredited Member*)—American Society of Appraisers designation.

Amortization—(1) the paying off of debt in regular installments over a period of time. (2) the deduction of capital expenses over a specific period of time (usually over the asset's life). More specifically, this method measures the consumption of the value of intangible assets, such as a patent or a copyright. (*investopedia.com*)

Appraisal—see **Valuation.**

Appraisal approach—see **Valuation approach.**

Appraisal date—see **Valuation date.**

Appraisal method—see **Valuation method.**

Appraisal procedure—see **Valuation procedure.**

Arbitrage pricing theory—a multivariate model for estimating the cost of equity capital, which incorporates several systematic risk factors.

ASA (*Accredited Senior Appraiser*)—American Society of Appraisers designation.

Asset (asset-based) approach—a general way of determining a value indication of a business, business ownership interest, or security using one or more methods based on the value of the assets net of liabilities.

AVA (*Accredited Valuation Analyst*)—National Association of Certified Valuation Analysts designation.

Average revenue per unit (ARPU)—a measure of the revenue generated per user or unit. This measure allows for the analysis of a company's revenue generation and growth at the per-unit level, which can identify which products are high or low revenue generators. (*investopedia.com*)

Beta—a measure of systematic risk of a stock; the tendency of a stock's price to correlate with changes in a specific index.

Binomial options pricing model (BOPM)—in finance, the binomial options pricing model (BOPM) provides a generalizable numerical method for the valuation of options. The binomial pricing model uses a "discrete-time framework" to trace the evolution of the option's key underlying variable via a binomial lattice (tree) for a given number of time steps between valuation date and option expiration. Each node in the lattice represents a possible price of the underlying at a particular point in time. This price evolution forms the basis for the option valuation. The valuation process is iterative, starting at each final node and then working backward through the tree to the first node (valuation date), where the calculated result is the value of the option. (*wikipedia.org*)

Binomial tree—a graphical representation of possible intrinsic values that an option may take at different nodes or time periods. The value of the option depends on the underlying stock or bond, and the value of the option at any node depends on the probability that the price of the underlying asset will either decrease or increase at any given node. (*investopedia.com*)

Black-Scholes option pricing model—a model of price variation over time of financial instruments such as stocks that can, among other things, be used to determine the price of a European call option. The model assumes that the price of heavily traded assets follow a geometric Brownian motion with constant drift and volatility. When applied to a stock option, the model incorporates the constant price variation of the stock, the time value of money, the option's strike price, and the time to the option's expiry. (*investopedia.com*)

Blockage discount—an amount or percentage deducted from the current market price of a publicly traded stock to reflect the decrease in the per-share value of a block of stock that is of a size that could not be sold in a reasonable period of time given normal trading volume.

Book value—see **Net book value.**

Business—see **Business enterprise.**

Business enterprise—a commercial, industrial, service, or investment entity (or a combination thereof) pursuing an economic activity.

Business risk—the degree of uncertainty of realizing expected future returns of the business resulting from factors other than financial leverage. See **Financial risk.**

Business valuation—the act or process of determining the value of a business enterprise or ownership interest therein.

Capital asset pricing model (CAPM)—a model in which the cost of capital for any stock or portfolio of stocks equals a risk-free rate plus a risk premium that is proportionate to the systematic risk of the stock or portfolio.

Capitalization—a conversion of a single period of economic benefits into value.

Capitalization factor—any multiple or divisor used to convert anticipated economic benefits of a single period into value.

Capitalization of earnings method—a method within the income approach whereby economic benefits for a representative single period are converted to value through division by a capitalization rate.

Capitalization rate—any divisor (usually expressed as a percentage) used to convert anticipated economic benefits of a single period into value.

Capital structure—the composition of the invested capital of a business enterprise, the mix of debt, and equity financing.

Cash flow—cash that is generated over a period of time by an asset, group of assets, or business enterprise. It may be used in a general sense to encompass various levels of specifically defined cash flows. When the term is used, it should be supplemented by a qualifier (for example, "discretionary" or "operating") and a specific definition in the given valuation context.

CBI (*Certified Business Intermediary*)—International Business Brokers Association designation.

CBV (*Chartered Business Valuator*)—Canadian Institute of Chartered Business Valuators designation.

CEIV (*Certified in Entity and Intangible Valuations*)—a credential for professionals performing fair value measurements for corporate entities and intangible assets. *(ceiv-credential.org)*

CFA (*Chartered Financial Analyst*)—CFA Institute designation.

CFF (*Certified in Financial Forensics*)—American Institute of Certified Public Accountants designation.

CFFA (*Certified Financial Forensic Analyst*)—National Association of Certified Valuation Analysts designation.

Coefficient of variation (CV)—a statistical measure of the dispersion of data points in a data series around the mean. It is calculated as follows: coefficient of variation = standard deviation/expected return. The coefficient of variation represents the ratio of the standard deviation to the mean, and it is a useful statistic for comparing the degree of variation from one data series to another, even if the means are drastically different from each other. (*investopedia.com*)

Common size statements—financial statements in which each line is expressed as a percentage of the total. On the balance sheet, each line item is shown as a percentage of total assets, and, on the income statement, each item is expressed as a percentage of sales.

Company specific risk (as defined by Butler Pinkerton model)—the portion of total risk specific to an individual asset that can be avoided through diversification. (*www.bvresources.com*)

Compound annual growth rate (CAGR)—the year-over-year growth rate of an investment over a specified period of time. The compound annual growth rate is calculated by taking the nth root of the total percentage growth rate, where n is the number of years in the period being considered. This can be written as follows: CAGR = [(ending value/ beginning value) ^ (1/number of years)] - 1. (*investopedia.com*)

Control—the power to direct the management and policies of a business enterprise.

Control premium—an amount or a percentage by which the pro rata value of a controlling interest exceeds the pro rata value of a noncontrolling interest in a business enterprise to reflect the power of control.

Cost approach—a general way of determining a value indication of an individual asset by quantifying the amount of money required to replace the future service capability of that asset.

Cost of capital—the expected rate of return that the market requires in order to attract funds to a particular investment.

Cost of goods sold—The direct costs attributable to the production of the goods sold by a company. This amount includes the cost of the materials used in creating the good along with the direct labor costs used to produce the good. It excludes indirect expenses such as distribution costs and sales force costs. COGS appears on the income statement and can be deducted from revenue to calculate a company's gross margin. (*investopedia.com*)

CPA/ABV (*CPA Accredited in Business Valuation*)—American Institute of Certified Public Accountants designation.

Current ratio—a liquidity ratio that measures a company's ability to pay short-term obligations. the current ratio formula is: current ratio = current assets/current liabilities. Also known as "liquidity ratio," "cash asset ratio," and "cash ratio." (*investopedia.com*)

CVA (*Certified Valuation Analyst*)—National Association of Certified Valuation Analysts designation.

Debt-free—*we discourage the use of this term.* See **Invested capital.**

Depreciation—in accounting, an expense recorded to allocate a tangible asset's cost over its useful life. Because depreciation is a noncash expense, it increases free cash flow while decreasing reported earnings. (*investopedia.com*)

Discount for lack of control—an amount or percentage deducted from the pro rata share of value of 100% of an equity interest in a business to reflect the absence of some or all of the powers of control.

Discount for lack of marketability—an amount or percentage deducted from the value of an ownership interest to reflect the relative absence of marketability.

Discount for lack of voting rights—an amount or percentage deducted from the per-share value of a minority interest voting share to reflect the absence of voting rights.

Discount rate—a rate of return used to convert a future monetary sum into present value.

Discounted cash flow method—a method within the income approach whereby the present value of future expected net cash flows is calculated using a discount rate.

Discounted future earnings method—a method within the income approach whereby the present value of future expected economic benefits is calculated using a discount rate.

Discretionary earnings—(as defined by *Pratt's Stats*) operating profit + owner's compensation + [depreciation/amortization] (*www.bvresources.com*)

Dividend yield—a financial ratio that shows how much a company pays out in dividends each year relative to its share price. In the absence of any capital gains, the dividend yield is the return on investment for a stock. Dividend yield is calculated as follows: annual dividends per share/price per share. (*investopedia.com*)

Earnings before interest and tax (EBIT)—an indicator of a company's profitability, calculated as revenue minus expenses, excluding tax and interest. EBIT is also referred to as "operating earnings," "operating profit," and "operating income," as you can rearrange the formula to be calculated as follows: EBIT = revenue - operating expenses. Also known as profit before interest and taxes (PBIT) and equals net income with interest and taxes added back to it. (*investopedia.com*)

Earnings before interest, taxes, depreciation, and amortization (EBITDA)—an indicator of a company's financial performance that is calculated in the following EBITDA calculation: EBITDA = revenue - expenses (excluding tax, interest, depreciation, and amortization). EBITDA is essentially net income with interest, taxes, depreciation, and amortization added back to it. EBITDA can be used to analyze and compare profitability between companies and industries because it eliminates the effects of financing and accounting decisions. However, this is a non-GAAP measure that allows a greater amount of discretion as to what is (and is not) included in the calculation. This also means that companies often change the items included in their EBITDA calculation from one reporting period to the next. (*investopedia.com*)

Economic benefits—inflows such as revenues, net income, net cash flows, etc.

Economic life—the period of time over which property may generate economic benefits.

Effective date—see **Valuation date.**

Employee stock ownership plan (ESOP)—a qualified, defined contribution, employee benefit (ERISA) plan designed to invest primarily in the stock of the sponsoring employer. ESOPs are "qualified" in the sense that the ESOP's sponsoring company, the selling shareholder, and participants receive various tax benefits. ESOPs are often used as a corporate finance strategy and are also used to align the interests of a company's employees with those of the company's shareholders. (*investopedia.com*)

Enterprise—see **Business enterprise.**

Equity—the owner's interest in property after deduction of all liabilities.

Equity net cash flows—those cash flows available to pay out to equity holders (in the form of dividends) after funding operations of the business enterprise, making necessary capital investments, and increasing or decreasing debt financing.

Equity risk premium—a rate of return added to a risk-free rate to reflect the additional risk of equity instruments over risk-free instruments (a component of the cost of equity capital or equity discount rate).

Excess earnings—that amount of anticipated economic benefits that exceeds an appropriate rate of return on the value of a selected asset base (often net tangible assets) used to generate those anticipated economic benefits.

Excess earnings method—a specific way of determining a value indication of a business, business ownership interest, or security determined as the sum of: (a) the value of the assets derived by capitalizing excess earnings; and (b) the value of the selected asset base. Also frequently used to value intangible assets. See **Excess earnings.**

Fair market value—the price, expressed in terms of cash equivalents, at which property would change hands between a hypothetical willing and able buyer and a hypothetical willing and able seller, acting at arm's length in an open and unrestricted market, when neither is under compulsion to buy or sell and when both have reasonable knowledge of the relevant facts. *(Note: In Canada, the term "price" should be replaced with the term "highest price.")*

Fair value—the value of the shares immediately before the effectuation of the corporate action to which the shareholder objects using customary and current valuation concepts and techniques generally employed for similar businesses in the context of the transaction requiring appraisal and without discounting for lack of marketability or minority status except, if appropriate, for amendments to the certificate of incorporation pursuant to section 13.02(a)(5). (*Revised Model Business Corporation Act* (RMBCA), American Bar Association (1999))

Fairness opinion—an opinion as to whether or not the consideration in a transaction is fair from a financial point of view.

Family limited partnership (FLP)—a type of partnership designed to centralize family business or investment accounts. FLPs pool together a family's assets into one single family-owned business partnership that family members own shares of. FLPs are frequently used as an estate tax minimization strategy, as shares in the FLP can be transferred between generations at lower taxation rates than would be applied to the partnership's holdings. (*investopedia.com*)

FASA (*Fellow of the American Society of Appraisers*)—American Society of Appraisers designation.

FCBI (*Fellow Certified Business Intermediary*)—International Business Brokers Association designation.

FCBV (***Fellow of the Canadian Institute of Chartered Business Valuators***)—Canadian Institute of Chartered Business Valuators designation.

Financial risk—the degree of uncertainty of realizing expected future returns of the business resulting from financial leverage. See **Business risk.**

Fixed assets—(as defined by *Pratt's Stats*) All property, plant, leasehold improvements, and equipment, net of accumulated depreciation or depletion. (www.bvresources.com)

Fixed asset turnover—a financial ratio of net sales to fixed assets. The fixed-asset turnover ratio measures a company's ability to generate net sales from fixed-asset investments—specifically property, plant, and equipment (PP&E)—net of depreciation. A higher fixed-asset turnover ratio shows that the company has been more effective in using the investment in fixed assets to generate revenues. The fixed-asset turnover ratio is calculated as: fixed asset turnover = net sales/net property, plant, and equipment. (*investopedia.com*)

Fixed charge coverage—(as defined by *Pratt's Stats*) operating profit/interest expense. (*www.bvresources.com*)

Forced liquidation value—liquidation value, at which the asset or assets are sold as quickly as possible, such as at an auction.

Free cash flow—***we discourage the use of this term.*** See **Net cash flows.**

Going concern—an ongoing operating business enterprise.

Going-concern value—the value of a business enterprise that is expected to continue to operate into the future. The intangible elements of going-concern value result from factors such as having a trained work force, an operational plant, and the necessary licenses, systems, and procedures in place.

Goodwill—that intangible asset arising as a result of name, reputation, customer loyalty, location, products, and similar factors not separately identified.

Goodwill value—the value attributable to goodwill.

Gross profit—a company's revenue minus its cost of goods sold. Gross profit is a company's residual profit after selling a product or service and deducting the cost associated with its production and sale. To calculate gross profit, examine the income statement, take the revenue, and subtract the cost of goods sold. Also called "gross margin" and "gross income." (*investopedia.com*)

Gross profit margin—a financial metric used to assess a firm's financial health by revealing the proportion of money left over from revenues after accounting for the cost of goods sold. Gross profit margin serves as the source for paying additional expenses and future savings. Also known as "gross margin." Calculated as: gross profit margin = (revenue - COGS)/revenue. (*investopedia.com*)

Guideline public company method—a method within the market approach whereby market multiples are derived from market prices of stocks of companies that are engaged in the same or similar lines of business and that are actively traded on a free and open market.

Holding period (as defined by the *Stout Restricted Stock Study*)—the amount of time the restricted stock must be held, based on the SEC rulings at the time of the restricted stock transaction. (*www.bvresources.com*)

Implied minority discount (as defined by the *FactSet Mergerstat/BVR Control Premium Study*)—an implied discount computed from the Mergerstat unaffected control premium. Calculated as: implied control premium = 1 - [1/(1 + control premium)]. (*Note: The Mergerstat unaffected control premium is the target company's common stock price per share unaffected by the acquisition announcement and is selected by Mergerstat after analyzing each transaction*). (*www.bvresources.com*)

Income (income-based) approach—a general way of determining a value indication of a business, business ownership interest, security, or intangible asset using one or more methods that convert anticipated economic benefits into a present single amount.

International Institute of Business Valuers (iiBV)—an organization that provides educational opportunities, promotes consistent professional ethics and standards, and facilitates the exchange of information and ideas for the business valuation profession globally. *(www.iibv.org)*

Intangible assets—nonphysical assets such as franchises, trademarks, patents, copyrights, goodwill, equities, mineral rights, securities, and contracts (as distinguished from physical assets) that grant rights and privileges and have value for the owner.

Internal rate of return—a discount rate at which the present value of the future cash flows of the investment equals the cost of the investment.

International Valuation Standards Council (IVSC)—a nonprofit organization that acts as a standards setter for valuation practice and the valuation profession. *(www.ivsc.org)*

Intrinsic value—the value that an investor considers, on the basis of an evaluation or available facts, to be the "true" or "real" value that will become the market value when other investors reach the same conclusion. When the term applies to options, it is the difference between the exercise price or strike price of an option and the market value of the underlying security.

Inventory turnover—a ratio showing how many times a company's inventory is sold and replaced over a period. Generally calculated as: sales/inventory. However, it may also be calculated as: cost of goods sold/average inventory. The days in the period can then be divided by the inventory turnover formula to calculate the days it takes to sell the inventory on hand or "inventory turnover days." (*investopedia.com*)

Invested capital—the sum of equity and debt in a business enterprise. Debt is typically: (a) all interest-bearing debt; or (b) long-term interest-bearing debt. When the term is used, it should be supplemented by a specific definition in the given valuation context.

Invested capital net cash flows—those cash flows available to pay out to equity holders (in the form of dividends) and debt investors (in the form of principal and interest) after funding operations of the business enterprise and making necessary capital investments.

Investment risk—the degree of uncertainty as to the realization of expected returns.

Investment value—the value to a particular investor based on individual investment requirements and expectations. (*Note: In Canada, the term used is "value to the owner."*)

Key person discount—an amount or percentage deducted from the value of an ownership interest to reflect the reduction in value resulting from the actual or potential loss of a key person in a business enterprise.

Levered beta—the beta reflecting a capital structure that includes debt.

Limited appraisal—the act or process of determining the value of a business, business ownership interest, security, or intangible asset with limitations in analyses, procedures, or scope.

Liquidity—the ability to quickly convert property to cash or pay a liability.

Liquidation value—the net amount that would be realized if the business is terminated and the assets are sold piecemeal. Liquidation can be either "orderly" or "forced."

Long-term liabilities—Recorded on the balance sheet, a company's liabilities for leases, bond repayments, and other items due in more than one year. (*investopedia.com*)

Majority control—the degree of control provided by a majority position.

Majority interest—an ownership interest greater than 50% of the voting interest in a business enterprise.

Market (market-based) approach—a general way of determining a value indication of a business, business ownership interest, security, or intangible asset by using one or more methods that compare the subject to similar businesses, business ownership interests, securities, or intangible assets that have been sold.

Market capitalization of equity—the share price of a publicly traded stock multiplied by the number of shares outstanding.

Market capitalization of invested capital—the market capitalization of equity plus the market value of the debt component of invested capital.

Market multiple—the market value of a company's stock or invested capital divided by a company measure (such as economic benefits, number of customers).

Market value of invested capital (MVIC) (as defined by Pratt's Stats)—also known as the selling price, the MVIC is defined by *Pratt's Stats* as the total consideration paid to the seller and includes any cash, notes, and/or securities that were used as a form of payment plus any interest-bearing liabilities assumed by the buyer. The MVIC price includes the noncompete value and the assumption of interest-bearing liabilities and excludes: (1) the real estate value; (2) any earnouts (because they have not yet been earned, and they may not be earned); and (3) the employment/consulting agreement values. (*www.bvresources.com*)

Marketability—the ability to quickly convert property to cash at minimal cost.

Marketability discount—see **Discount for lack of marketability.**

Merger and acquisition method—a method within the market approach whereby pricing multiples are derived from transactions of significant interests in companies engaged in the same or similar lines of business.

Midyear discounting—a convention used in the discounted future earnings method that reflects economic benefits being generated at midyear, approximating the effect of economic benefits being generated evenly throughout the year.

Minority discount—a discount for lack of control applicable to a minority interest.

Minority interest—an ownership interest less than 50% of the voting interest in a business enterprise.

Multiple—the inverse of the capitalization rate.

NAICS code—see **North American Industry Classification System.**

Net book value—with respect to a business enterprise, the difference between total assets (net of accumulated depreciation, depletion, and amortization) and total liabilities as they appear on the balance sheet (synonymous with shareholder's equity). With respect to a specific asset, the capitalized cost less accumulated amortization or depreciation as it appears on the books of account of the business enterprise.

Net cash flows—when the term is used, it should be supplemented by a qualifier. See **Equity, Net cash flows,** and **Invested capital net cash flows.**

Net income—a company's total earnings (or profit). Net income is calculated by taking revenues and adjusting for the cost of doing business, depreciation, interest, taxes, and other expenses. This number is found on a company's income statement and is an important measure of how profitable the company is over a period of time. The measure is also used to calculate earnings per share. Often referred to as "the bottom line" since net income is listed at the bottom of the income statement. In the U.K., net income is known as "profit attributable to shareholders." (*investopedia.com*)

Net operating profit after tax (NOPAT)—a company's potential cash earnings if its capitalization were unleveraged (that is, if it had no debt). NOPAT is frequently used in economic value added (EVA) calculations. Calculated as: NOPAT = operating income × (1 - tax rate). (*investopedia.com*)

Net present value—the value, as of a specified date, of future cash inflows less all cash outflows (including the cost of investment) calculated using an appropriate discount rate.

Net profit margin—the ratio of net profits to revenues for a company or business segment—typically expressed as a percentage—that shows how much of each dollar earned by the company is translated into profits. Net profit margins can generally be calculated as: net profit margin = net profit/revenue; where net profit = revenue - COGS - operating expenses - interest and taxes. (*investopedia.com*)

Net tangible asset value—the value of the business enterprise's tangible assets (excluding excess assets and nonoperating assets) minus the value of its liabilities.

Net worth—The amount by which assets exceed liabilities. This term can be applied to companies and individuals. (*investopedia.com*)

Noncash charges—Noncash charges are typically against the depreciation, amortization, and depletion accounts on a company's balance sheet. Companies take these charges against earnings due to extraordinary circumstances such as accounting policy changes or significant depreciation of asset's market value. (*investopedia.com*)

Nonoperating assets—assets not necessary to ongoing operations of the business enterprise. (*Note: In Canada, the term used is "redundant assets."*)

Normalized earnings—economic benefits adjusted for nonrecurring, noneconomic, or other unusual items to eliminate anomalies and/or facilitate comparisons.

Normalized financial statements—financial statements adjusted for nonoperating assets and liabilities and/or for nonrecurring, noneconomic, or other unusual items to eliminate anomalies and/or facilitate comparisons.

North American Industry Classification System (NAICS)—used by business and government to classify and measure economic activity in Canada, Mexico, and the United States. It has largely replaced the older Standard Industrial Classification (SIC) system; however, certain government departments and agencies, such as the U.S. Securities and Exchange Commission (SEC), still use the SIC codes. (*wikipedia.org*)

Operating expenses—A category of expenditure that a business incurs as a result of performing its normal business operations. One of the typical responsibilities that management must contend with is determining how low operating expenses can be reduced without significantly affecting the firm's ability to compete with its competitors. (*investopedia.com*)

Operating profit—the amount of profit realized from a business's own operations, but excluding operating expenses (such as cost of goods sold) and depreciation from gross income. Also known as "earnings before interest and tax" (EBIT). Calculated as: operating profit = revenue - COGS - operating expenses - depreciation and amortization. (*investopedia.com*)

Operating profit margin—a ratio used to measure a company's pricing strategy and operating efficiency. Calculated as: operating profit margin = operating income/revenue. Operating profit margin is a measurement of what proportion of a company's revenue is left over after paying for variable costs of production such as wages, raw materials, etc. A healthy operating margin is required for a company to be able to pay for its fixed costs, such as interest on debt. Also known as "operating margin." (*investopedia.com*)

Orderly liquidation value—liquidation value at which the asset or assets are sold over a reasonable period of time to maximize proceeds received.

Outstanding shares—stock currently held by investors, including restricted shares owned by the company's officers and insiders, as well as those held by the public. Shares that have been repurchased by the company are not considered outstanding stock. (*investopedia.com*)

Premise of value—an assumption regarding the most likely set of transactional circumstances that may be applicable to the subject valuation, e.g., going concern, liquidation.

Present value—the value, as of a specified date, of future economic benefits and/or proceeds from sale, calculated using an appropriate discount rate.

Price/earnings multiple—the price of a share of stock divided by its earnings per share.

Private placement—the raising of capital via private rather than public placement. The result is the sale of securities to a relatively small number of investors. Investors involved in private placements are usually large banks, mutual funds, insurance companies, and pension funds. (*investopedia.com*)

Portfolio discount—an amount or percentage deducted from the value of a business enterprise to reflect the fact that it owns dissimilar operations or assets that do not fit well together.

Quick ratio—an indicator of a company's short-term liquidity. The quick ratio measures a company's ability to meet its short-term obligations with its most liquid assets. The higher the quick ratio, the better the position of the company. The quick ratio is calculated as: quick ratio = (current assets - inventories)/current liabilities. Also known as the "acid-test ratio" or the "quick assets ratio." (*investopedia.com*)

Rate of return—an amount of income (loss) and/or change in value realized or anticipated on an investment, expressed as a percentage of that investment.

Redundant assets—see **Nonoperating assets.**

Recurring revenue—the portion of a company's revenue that is highly likely to continue in the future. This is revenue that is predictable, stable, and can be counted on in the future with a high degree of certainty. (*investopedia.com*)

Report date—the date conclusions are transmitted to the client.

Replacement cost new—the current cost of a similar new property having the nearest equivalent utility to the property being valued.

Reproduction cost new—the current cost of an identical new property.

Required rate of return—the minimum rate of return acceptable by investors before they will commit money to an investment at a given level of risk.

Residual value—the value as of the end of the discrete projection period in a discounted future earnings model.

Restricted stock—restricted stock, also known as letter stock or restricted securities, refers to stock of a company that is not fully transferable until certain conditions have been met. Upon satisfaction of those conditions, the stock becomes transferable by the person holding the award. (*wikipedia.org*)

Retained earnings—the percentage of net earnings not paid out as dividends, but retained by the company to be reinvested in its core business or to pay debt. It is recorded under shareholders' equity on the balance sheet. The formula calculates retained earnings by adding net income to (or subtracting any net losses from) beginning retained earnings and subtracting any dividends paid to shareholders: retained earnings = beginning retained earnings + net income - dividends. (*investopedia.com*)

Return on assets (ROA)—an indicator of how profitable a company is relative to its total assets. ROA gives an idea as to how efficient management is at using its assets to generate earnings. Calculated by dividing a company's annual earnings by its total assets, ROA is displayed as a percentage. (*investopedia.com*)

Return on equity—the amount, expressed as a percentage, earned on a company's common equity for a given period.

Return on investment—see **Return on invested capital** and **Return on equity.**

Return on invested capital—the amount, expressed as a percentage, earned on a company's total capital for a given period.

Return on revenue (ROR)—a measure of a corporation's profitability, calculated as net income divided by revenue. (*investopedia.com*)

Revenue—the amount of money that a company actually receives during a specific period, including discounts and deductions for returned merchandise. It is the "top line" or "gross income" figure from which costs are subtracted to determine net income. Revenue is calculated by multiplying the price at which goods or services are sold by the number of units or amount sold. (*investopedia.com*)

Risk-free rate—the rate of return available in the market on an investment free of default risk.

Risk premium—a rate of return added to a risk-free rate to reflect risk.

Rule 144—promulgated by the SEC under the 1933 Act, Rule 144 permits, under limited circumstances, the sale of restricted and controlled securities without registration. In addition to restrictions on the minimum length of time for which such securities must be held and the maximum volume permitted to be sold, the issuer must agree to the sale. If certain requirements are met, Form 144 must be filed with the SEC. Often, the issuer requires that a legal opinion be given indicating that the resale complies with the rule. (*wikipedia.org*)

Rule of thumb—a mathematical formula developed from the relationship between price and certain variables based on experience, observation, hearsay, or a combination of these; usually industry specific.

SDE—see **Seller's discretionary earnings.**

Seller's discretionary earnings (as defined by *BIZCOMPS*)—calculated by adding to the most recent full year's net income before taxes (NIBT): amortization, depreciation, interest, owner's compensation, owner's benefits, non-business-related expenses, and one-time-only expenses. Normally to one working owner. (*www.bvresources.com*)

Size premium—size premium is the additional remuneration due to the higher risk and, therefore, the higher cost of capital, associated with the smaller size of the company and of the lower trading volume. (*vernimmen.com*)

Special interest purchasers—acquirers who believe they can enjoy post-acquisition economies of scale, synergies, or strategic advantages by combining the acquired business interest with their own.

Standard Industrial Classification (SIC)—a United States government system for classifying industries by a four-digit code. (*wikipedia.org*)

Standard of value—the identification of the type of value being used in a specific engagement, e.g., fair market value, fair value, investment value.

Stockholders' equity—The portion of the balance sheet that represents the capital received from investors in exchange for stock (paid-in capital), donated capital, and retained earnings. Stockholders' equity represents the equity stake currently held on the books by a firm's equity investors. It is calculated either as a firm's total assets minus its total liabilities or as share capital plus retained earnings minus Treasury shares. (*investopedia.com*)

Strike price—the price at which a specific derivative contract can be exercised. Strike price is mostly used to describe stock and index options, in which strike prices are fixed in the contract. For call options, the strike price is where the security can be bought (up to the expiration date), while for put options the strike price is the price at which shares can be sold. The difference between the underlying security's current market price and the option's strike price represents the amount of profit per share gained upon the exercise or the sale of the option. This is true for options that are in the money; the maximum amount that can be lost is the premium paid. Also known as the "exercise price." (*investopedia.com*)

Sustaining capital reinvestment—the periodic capital outlay required to maintain operations at existing levels, net of the tax shield available from such outlays.

Systematic risk—the risk that is common to all risky securities and cannot be eliminated through diversification. The measure of systematic risk in stocks is the beta coefficient.

Tangible assets—physical assets (such as cash; accounts receivable; inventory; property, plant, and equipment, etc.).

Target invested capital (as defined by *Mergerstat/BVR Control Premium Study*)—target company's implied total invested capital (TIC) based on the sum of the implied market value of equity (the purchase price per share times total shares outstanding reported in the period prior to the transaction's announcement date) plus the face value of total interest-bearing debt and the book value of preferred stock outstanding prior to the announcement date. (*www.bvresources.com*)

Terminal value. see **Residual value.**

Total asset turnover—this is a measure of how well assets are being used to produce revenue. The total asset turnover ratio is calculated as: total asset turnover = net sales/ total assets. (*investorwords.com*)

Total beta—total beta is equal to the identity: beta/R or the standard deviation of the stock/standard deviation of the market (*note: the relative volatility*). Total beta captures the security's risk as a stand-alone asset (since the correlation coefficient, R, has been removed from beta), rather than part of a well-diversified portfolio. Since appraisers frequently value closely held companies as stand-alone assets, total beta is gaining acceptance in the business valuation industry. Appraisers can now use total beta in the following equation: total cost of equity (TCOE) = risk-free rate + total beta*equity risk premium. Once appraisers have a number of TCOE benchmarks, they can compare/contrast the risk factors present in these publicly traded benchmarks and the risks in their closely held company to better defend/support their valuations. (*wikipedia.org*)

Total cost of equity (TCOE)—total cost of equity (TCOE) = risk-free rate + total beta*equity risk premium. This equation was developed by Professor Damodaran at New York University's Stern School of Business . For more information on total beta, see **Total beta.**

Transaction method—see **Merger and acquisition method.**

Unlevered beta—the beta reflecting a capital structure without debt.

Unsystematic risk—the risk specific to an individual security that can be avoided through diversification.

Valuation—the act or process of determining the value of a business, business ownership interest, security, or intangible asset.

Valuation approach—a general way of determining a value indication of a business, business ownership interest, security, or intangible asset using one or more valuation methods.

Valuation date—the specific point in time when the valuator's opinion of value applies (also referred to as "effective date" or "appraisal date").

Valuation method—within approaches, a specific way to determine value.

Valuation multiple—see **Valuation ratio.**

Valuation procedure—the act, manner, and technique of performing the steps of an appraisal method.

Valuation ratio—a fraction in which a value or price serves as the numerator and financial, operating, or physical data serve as the denominator.

Value to the owner—see **Investment value.**

Vesting period—In options, the remaining time period during which the option cannot be exercised. (*www.bvresources.com*)

VIX—see **Volatility index.**

Volatility index—VIX is the ticker symbol for the Chicago Board Options Exchange Volatility Index, a popular measure of the implied volatility of S&P 500 index options. A high value corresponds to a more volatile market and therefore more costly options, which can be used to defray risk from this volatility by selling options. Often referred to as the *fear index,* it represents one measure of the market's expectation of volatility over the next 30-day period. (*wikipedia.com*)

Voting control—de jure control of a business enterprise.

Weighted average cost of capital (WACC)—the cost of capital (discount rate) determined by the weighted average, at market value, of the cost of all financing sources in the business enterprise's capital structure.

Z-score—a statistical measure that quantifies the distance (measured in standard deviations) a data point is from the mean of a data set. In a more financial sense, Z-score is the output from a credit-strength test that gauges the likelihood of bankruptcy. A z-score of 0 is equal to a 50% probability of bankruptcy. (*investopedia.com*)

Appendix 11. *Business Valuation Bench Book* Questions

1. Under the facts and circumstances of the case, has the expert chosen the correct premise of value and standard of value?
2. Has the expert considered the market, income, and asset approaches and what is his or her support for using one approach over the other?
3. Does the expert have a thorough understanding of the business and has he or she considered the eight factors of Revenue Ruling 59-60?
4. Which expert has the more reasonable, understandable, and supportable adjustments to the income?
5. For the *reasonable compensation adjustment,* would a nonowner employee perform this work for this amount of money?
6. Why does the expert believe his or her determination of the normalized income to capitalize best represents the expected future performance of the company?
7. For the *cap rate,* has the expert adequately explained the components of discount rate, especially the specific company risk premium and the appropriate long-term growth rate in light of past performance, and the expected future performance, the economic and industry conditions?
8. Has the expert matched the income to the cap rate?
9. For the *DCF method,* why does the expert believe the (multiperiod) DCF method is more appropriate than the (single-period) capitalization of earnings method?
10. Under the DCF method, can revenues realistically grow at the projected rates and do the expenses support the revenues?
11. Does the discount rate for the DCF adequately present the risk of achieving the projected income?
12. For the *asset approach,* is this an asset holding entity or an asset-intensive business such as real estate, which is appropriate for the methodology?

13. For *excess earnings,* which expert provided the best documentation and explanation for:

    a. Return on net tangible assets; and

    b. Cap rate on excess earnings.

14. For the *market approach,* is the sale of assets or stock; for an asset sale, what assets are or are not included in the sales price?

15. Have appropriate adjustments been made to make the companies or transactions comparable?

Appendix 12. *Business Valuation Bench Book* Reference Guide

Premises of Value:

- *Value in exchange:* Owner realizes value by selling the business; and
- *Value to the holder:* Owner realizes the value of ownership by the cash flow received while owning the business.

Standards of Value:

- *Fair market value:* Value in exchange concept—business is valued assuming a hypothetical sale between a willing buyer and a willing seller if appropriate minority and marketability discounts are allowed; and
- *Fair value:* Similar to fair market value, but minority discounts are not applied and marketability discounts are only applied under extraordinary circumstances. Can include the value to the holder premise because the business cannot be sold or there is no intention to sell.

Business Valuation Approaches:

- *Market approach:* If you sell your house, you look at sales of houses similar to yours and make adjustments for amenities and other differences to arrive at an asking price;
- *Income approach:* If you rent your house, you can determine the value of your house by estimating the total rental income the house could generate over the years, assuming that a dollar today is worth more than a dollar in the future; and
- *Asset approach:* If you were to buy a new house, the builder would charge for the price of the land, the costs to construct the house, and a profit.

Normalized Earnings:

- Adjustments to revenue;
- Adjustments to expenses; and
- Reasonable compensation.

Capitalization Rate:

- Discount rate; and
- Long-term growth rate.

Discounted Cash Flow Method (DCF):

- Used when the expected future earnings cannot be represented by a single period—income in the immediate future is expected to differ from income in the past and long-term future.

Excess Earnings Method:

- Expert must determine rates of return for *net tangible assets* and *capitalization rate on the excess income*; and
- Value is computed as follows: net tangible assets + goodwill = value.

Market Approach:

- Value is calculated by comparing the business or business interest being valued with comparison transaction information from the company itself or guideline companies/transactions; and
- Based on the principle of substitution, which states that a prudent buyer will pay no more for a property than it would cost to acquire an equally desirable substitute.

CPSIA information can be obtained
at www.ICGtesting.com
Printed in the USA
BVOW05*2301050817
491128BV00006B/7/P